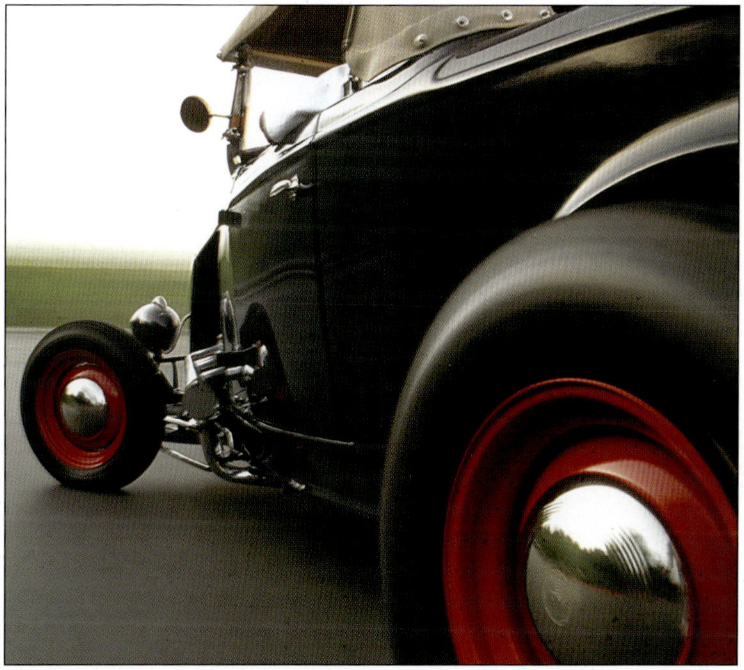

DEUCE
75 Years of the '32 Ford

Robert Genat

CarTech®

© 2006 by Robert Genat

All rights reserved. No part of this publication may be reproduced or utilized in any form or by any means, electronic or mechanical, including photocopying, recording, or by any information storage and retrieval system, without prior written permission from the author. All photos and artwork are the property of the author.

The information in this work is true and complete to the best of our knowledge. However, all information is presented without any guarantee on the part of the author or publisher, who also disclaim any liability incurred in connection with the use of the information.

The author and publisher recognize that some words, model names, and designations, for example, mentioned herein are the property of the trademark holder. We use them for identification purposes only. This is not an official publication of any of the firms mentioned.

Edited by Peter Bodensteiner

Designed by Katie Sonmor

ISBN-13 978-1-932494-13-6
ISBN-10 1-932494-13-8

Printed in China

CarTech®
39966 Grand Avenue
North Branch, MN 55056
Telephone: (651) 277-1200 or (800) 551-4754
Fax: (651) 277-1203
www.cartechbooks.com

Library of Congress Cataloging-in-Publication Data

Genat, Robert, 1945-
  Deuce, 75 years of the '32 Ford / by Robert Genat.
    p. cm.
   ISBN 1-932494-13-8
 1. Ford automobile--History--20th century. 2. Ford Model A automobile--History. 3. Antique and classic cars. 4. Hot rods--History. I. Title.

TL215.F35G46 2006
629.222'2--dc22

2006005326

Cover:
The 1932 Ford grille shell is one of the most recognizable elements of the car to either hot rodder or restorer. Its clean look was derived from Lincoln's similar grille shell. Another iconic element from the front of the car is the attractive headlight bar with the V-8 emblem in the center. The Deuce was the last Ford passenger car to have a headlight bar.

Back Cover:
Left:
Ford used a wooden framework to support the fixed roof insert on its sedan and coupe models. All of the top inserts were black vinyl.

Inset:
In the early 1970s a low-budget movie about cruising called American Graffiti and its star car, this chopped '32 coupe, helped hot rodding flourish once again.

Front Flap:
Jim Austin's five-window looks as though it could have come right out of the Ford factory, but the chopped top and rake give it away as a hot rod.

Frontis:
John Maynard's dark blue '32 Roadster has a slick set of headers sticking out of the engine compartment. Its stance is traditional hot rod with larger tires in the rear.

Title Page:
The 1932 Ford holds a special place in the hearts of both hot rodders and restorers. Its classic lines made it an icon of 1930s automotive styling and its new V-8 put Ford on the leading edge of engine development.

Endpapers:
Roadsters, especially '32 Ford highboys, have always been some of the most popular hot rods in Southern California. The state's moderate temperatures and good roads allow year-round use.

OVERSEAS DISTRIBUTION BY:

Brooklands Books Ltd.
P.O. Box 146, Cobham, Surrey, KT11 1LG, England
Telephone 01932 865051 • Fax 01932 868803
www.brooklands-books.com

Brooklands Books Aus.
3/37-39 Green Street, Banksmeadow, NSW 2109, Australia
Telephone 2 9695 7055 • Fax 2 9695 7355

Contents

Dedication		.6
Acknowledgments		.7
Introduction		.8
Chapter One:	The Fordmobile Through the Model A	.20
Chapter Two:	The New 1932 Ford	.28
Chapter Three:	The New V-8	.56
Chapter Four:	Ford's 1932 Open Cars: Roadsters, Phaetons & Cabriolets	.70
Chapter Five:	1932 Ford Coupes	.102
Chapter Six:	Ford's 1932 Sedans and Commercial Vehicles	.136
Chapter Seven:	The Future of the 1932 Ford	.170
Photo Credits		.189
Index		.190

Dedication

To Amber Trakul, my lovely godchild.

Don Prieto's '32 Roadster is fitted with a fiberglass body built by Harwood Industries. When Harwood built their molds, they increased the length of the door by 2 inches over the standard Ford body.

Acknowledgments

Thanks to my commissioning editor Steve Hendrickson for allowing me to take on this project. And thanks to the following people for their help during the process: Gary Jankowski, Pete Chapouris, Kenny Gollohan at Brookville Roadster, Tony Thacker at SoCal Speed Shop, Derek de Heras, David Newhardt, Gordie and Connie Craig, Lynn Stringer, George DeAngelis, John and Billy Couch, Bob Bauder, Greg Sharp, David Rehor, Barry Lobeck, Dain Gingerelli, "Speedy" Bill Smith of Speedway Motors, Janice Rudolph and Craig Knight of Hot Rods and Horsepower, Henry Astor of the American Hot Rod Foundation, Mark Kirby, Jim Orr and John Boden at the Benson Ford Research Center at the Henry Ford Museum, and Dick Messer and his staff at the Petersen Automotive Museum.

My thanks to the following car owners for their patience and understanding while I waited for the "right" light or had them reposition their car a dozen times while looking for the perfect angle. Their investment in time and money has preserved these wonderful cars. I especially thank those owners who took me for rides or let me drive their cars. It's a side benefit of this job I love. Thanks to: Henry Astor, Rick Cronin, Gordie and Connie Craig, Rick Figari, Linda Guinn, Ken Gross, Bruce Meyer, Lynn Stringer, Lew Wolff, Paul Gommi, Jon Hall, Don Carpenter, Bob Everets, Mark Mountanos, Chuck de Heras, Nick Alexander, David Boule, John Farrar, Fred Meyer, Randy Fish, Dean Ferrari, Curt Catallo, Julian Alvarez, Paul King, Don Prieto, Bill Couch, John Couch, Jerry and Sharon Stein, Roger Morrison, Bob Berry, Elwood Peterson, Rich Guasco, John Maynard, Phil Brooks, Dr. Mark VanBuskirk, Jerry Jacobson, Sam Davis, Jim Austin, and Jack Kuttner,

This book is intended to celebrate 75 years of the 1932 Ford. It is not intended as a 1932 Ford restoration guide nor is it a guide on how to build a 1932 Ford hot rod. I tried to find the best examples of original, un-restored, or fully restored 1932 Fords. I also looked for the 1932 Ford hot rods that best exemplify the art of hot rod building. I searched for interesting archival photography that would allow us to appreciate how wonderful these cars looked when they were first introduced. Some of the 1932 Fords in this book are original un-restored cars and some are flawless restorations. Some hot rods are rough around the edges and others are award winners. But, they're all 1932 Fords.

— *Robert Genat*

Introduction

The 1932 Ford was the stepping stone between the boxy Model As and the much sleeker '33 Ford. It offered the buyer of a mid-priced car V-8 power, a selling point Chevrolet or Plymouth could not match.

8 ■ DEUCE: 75 YEARS OF THE '32 FORD

INTRODUCTION

There is no car in hot-rodding history that has cast a bigger shadow than the 1932 Ford. When first introduced, it gave the American auto buyer the same level of luxury that larger and more expensive cars did 10 years earlier; its new V-8 engine was revolutionary. The 1932 Ford is also one of those rare anomalies in the auto industry—a one-year-only car. Automakers learned early on that releasing a new model and carrying it over for several years made good economic sense. Ford's Model T endured for 19 years and the Model A for 4 years. Designers typically changed or revised something each model year, but the basic package remained the same. Not so with the 1932 Ford. It stood alone between the boxy 1931 Model A and the sleek 1933 models. This oddity is compounded by the fact that in 1932, America was in the depths of the Great Depression.

Against all odds, delayed by production problems, and at the cost of millions of dollars, the 1932 Ford was introduced March 31, 1932. The interest created by the new, innovative V-8 brought 5.5 million people into showrooms in the debut week. Teething problems plagued Ford's early V-8s, but Henry Ford remained steadfast behind the V-8 engine and its potential to keep Ford cars ahead of the competition.

In the middle of a depression, it would seem that an automaker should pare back its number of models and concentrate on being efficient to survive. Ford went against conventional wisdom and produced 14 body styles that included two uniquely different coupes, a

While Ford's new 1932 models were attractive and well-built, sales faltered. One quarter of Americans were unemployed during the depression, and those who were working were uncomfortable spending their money on a new car.

9 ■ DEUCE: 75 YEARS OF THE '32 FORD

INTRODUCTION

To promote the new Ford, this 1/2-mile test track was created where salesmen could take prospective buyers for a ride. Ford Motor Company and its dealers pulled out all the stops in creating events to promote its cars in 1932.

regular two-door sedan (Deluxe and Standard), a Victoria sedan, and the sporty two-door Cabriolet and Sport Coupe models. All of these were available with either the 50-horsepower four-cylinder or 65-horsepower V-8. Sales reflected the country's poor economy with 1932 production numbers dropping to 266,613 units—only one-third the number of cars that Ford had produced a year earlier.

In 1933, a boldly styled Ford debuted with a sleek silhouette and refined V-8 engine. Sales still flagged due to the depression, but the outlook was brighter. In 1934, Ford production was over 500,000, but it would not

That's Mickey Rooney, and the character he is playing has just wrecked his 1932 Phaeton. The 1932 Ford was an exceptionally well-built car and, barring this kind of treatment, that's one reason why so many of them have survived.

10 ■ DEUCE: 75 YEARS OF THE '32 FORD

This mid-1930s era used car lot has several '32 sedans lined up on the left. Ford built more two-door sedans than any other body style.

Ford's new V-8 engine was revolutionary because of its monoblock design. Most other V-8 engines at that time used multi-piece blocks. Ford's inventive design was less expensive to manufacture and drove down the cost of a V-8 engine to help make it available to anyone.

regain the sales lead until 1935. Ford's trusty four-cylinder engine faded from memory; all Ford passenger cars, starting in 1935, were equipped with a V-8. Ford's new V-8 engine had successfully raised the bar for automakers.

When the first V-8 was introduced, it offered more power than the stock four-cylinder engine. It didn't have the immediate impact on the automotive world that the small-block Chevy engine did in 1955 or the Hemi did in 1966. In stock form, the V-8s were no match for highly modified four-cylinder Ford engines, which hot rodders had been tinkering with for years. Many aftermarket manufacturers made bolt-on components that substantially increased the four banger's horsepower. The new V-8 was intriguing, but without the aftermarket hop-up components, there was no fascination in starting all over again on the new V-8.

Continued on page 15

INTRODUCTION

The new Ford in the foreground is a Cabriolet and the one in the background is a Victoria sedan—two of the more upscale models Ford offered in 1932. Both of these models were only available in Deluxe trim.

INTRODUCTION

Ford offered its popular 1932 four-door sedan in both Standard and Deluxe trim. A scant few years earlier Ford only sold cars painted black. But by 1932, Ford offered several color combinations and the option of color-coordinated wheels.

Ford introduced two distinctly different coupes in 1932: a Standard five-window and this Deluxe three-window. The three-window was the only closed model in 1932 with a chrome windshield frame.

13 ■ DEUCE: 75 YEARS OF THE '32 FORD

INTRODUCTION

Every year someone opens an old barn and finds a well-preserved 1932 Ford hiding in a dusty corner. The fact that so many of these cars have survived is a testament to how well they were built and the affection the public had for them.

INTRODUCTION

The 1932 Ford Roadster has long been established as the most popular hot rod in the world. Its hot rod legacy started on California's dry lakes and continues today on streets all over America.

Hot rodders did like the new 1932 body styles and chassis. The only downside was the fact that the new body was physically larger than the Model A. A larger body meant more aerodynamic drag. And when it came to body styles, the only one that mattered to hot rodders was the roadster. The roadster had a wind-in-your-face, sporty élan, much like today's Vipers and Corvettes. Coupes and sedans were seen as family cars.

This bias toward roadsters was clearly evidenced by the Southern California Timing Association's (SCTA) lack of a coupe class for its time trials on California's dry lakes. Roadsters were also more prevalent in Southern California, where an open roadster could be driven year round. This abundance of good-looking roadsters, along with their initial lower cost, made the Ford Roadster the hot rodder's choice.

The Deuce Comes Into Its Own

Ford's new V-8 became popular with hot rodders just as World War II began. The hot rod world went on hold except in the fertile young minds of hot rodders. Those shipped off to war thought about hot rods and even tinkered with the engines in the jeeps they were driving during their military deployments. Those left behind to work in industry to support the war created new processes to build aircraft and tanks. In this way they honed their mechanical/hot rodding skills.

INTRODUCTION

In this roadster's heyday it was owned by three different owners: Bill Woodward, Neal East, and Bill Moeller. It was featured on the cover of the August 1961 edition of Rod & Custom *magazine and was photographed here at the 1962 Detroit Autorama. It's one of the best examples of a full-fendered '32 roadster ever built.*

When the war ended and the soldiers came home, hot rodding exploded. In addition to returning native Californians, there were those transplants who were either trained or stationed in California during the war. Many more who grew up in the Midwest or East heard the stories from their military buddies of driving at full speed across California's dry lakes and came out for a new adventure. Fueling this demand was the wealth of

The coupe that John Milner drove in the movie American Graffiti *reminded everyone how great a simple hot rod could be. At the time that movie was released, America had lost sight of its hot rod roots and was distracted by customized vans and Volkswagens. This yellow coupe snapped us back to reality.*

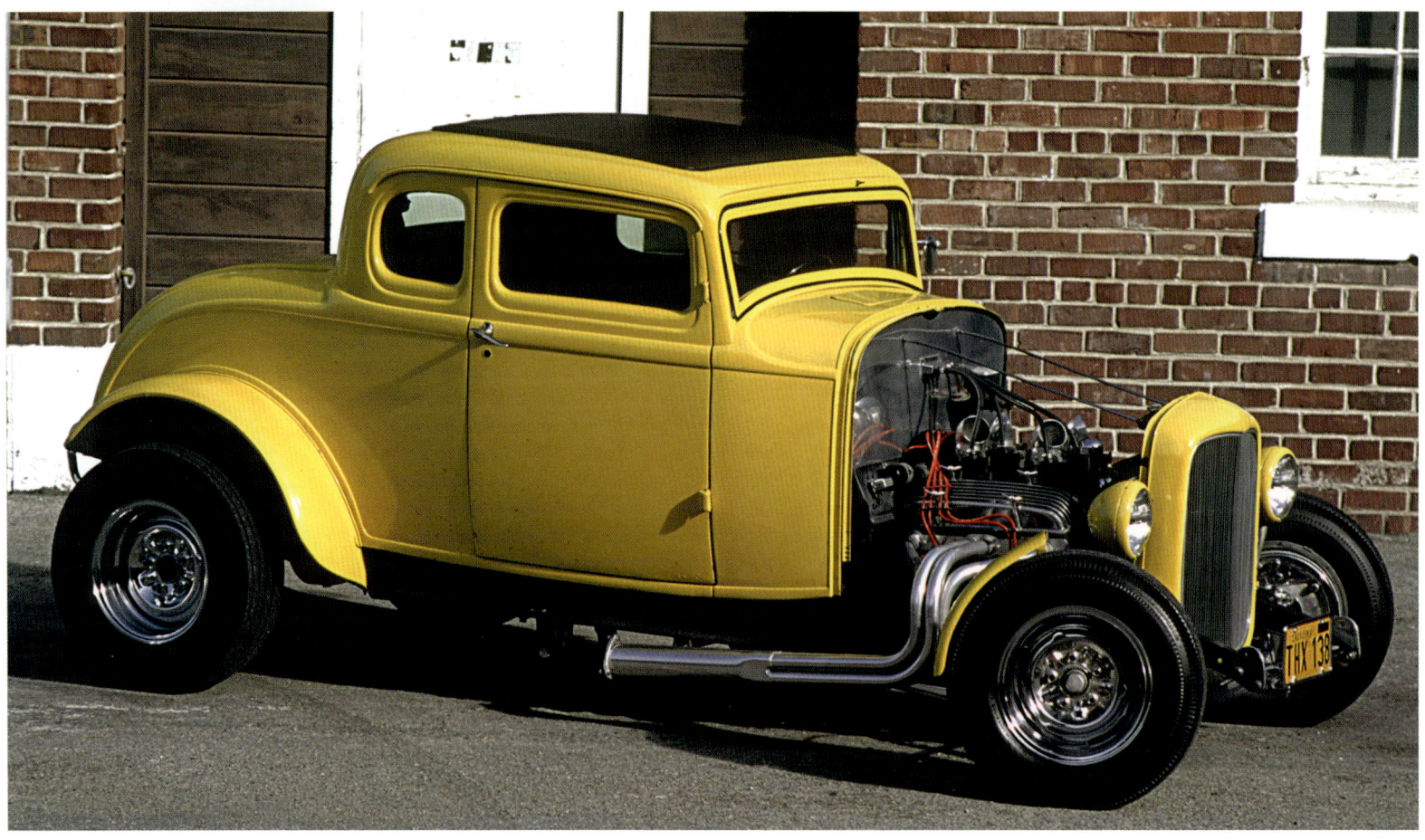

16 ■ DEUCE: 75 YEARS OF THE '32 FORD

INTRODUCTION

One of hot rodding's icon cars is Clarence "Chili" Catallo's '32 Coupe. It bridged the worlds of hot rodding and custom cars.

available early Ford cars in California. With new car production in full swing, many mainstream car buyers were glad to get rid of their 1930s-era Ford for something new. Hot rodders were there ready to accept the cast-off cars and parts.

Many soldiers returning from military service had learned to maintain all types of aircraft. They brought their exciting skill-sets to hot rodding. They now knew about specialized fasteners, how to work with and weld aluminum, supercharging techniques, and how to build strong frame structures. At military surplus houses, hot rodders could buy aircraft-grade fasteners, aluminum bucket seats, seat belts, and belly tanks.

This surge of hot rodding activity spurred the development of the Ford flathead V-8 as a performance engine. Hot rodding visionaries like Vic Edelbrock developed heads and intake manifolds, while others zeroed in on cam grinding and ignition systems. With a little work, Henry's little flathead came to life and the hot rodding world swirled around it as the cornerstone of performance.

Hot rod '32 coupes have found their own niche in the world of hot rodding. The proportions of David Boule's chopped three-window are exceptionally pleasing to the eye, especially when combined with the appropriate tire size and aggressive nose-down rake.

DEUCE: 75 YEARS OF THE '32 FORD

INTRODUCTION

Hot rodding had its ups and downs after that, but the '32 Ford always remained a focal point of interest, even during the mid-to-late 1960s when muscle cars were all the rage, and during the 1970s when production cars became forgettable. The 1972 movie *American Graffiti* reminded people of what fun they used to have cruising Main Street in their own towns. The hot rod freed them from the monotony of 55 mile-per-hour speed limits, catalytic converters, and stodgy, cookie-cutter cars lacking in personality.

Ford only built 210,824 1932 Fords. To satisfy the demand of the hot rod market, several companies are building fiberglass reproduction bodies and chassis. With the exception of the original 1932 California license plate, this entire 1932 five-window coupe is built from reproduction parts. Now every hot rodder can have the car of his or her dreams.

With the reproduction parts available today, a garage filled with cars like these is within the reach of many hot rodders. In addition, the quality and variety of components has vastly improved.

18 ■ DEUCE: 75 YEARS OF THE '32 FORD

INTRODUCTION

The 1932 Ford highboy roadster remains as the quintessential American hot rod. The stylish body and unique frame set it apart from all of the others cars built in 1932. It was the car that early hot rodders fell in love with, and the love affair has lasted 75 years.

The resurgence in hot rodding created the demand for more 1932 Fords. The first body to be elegantly reproduced in fiberglass was the roadster. Next came coupes and sedans. Even new "phantom" body styles have been created. The lack of original frames was also a challenge met by the aftermarket industry. Today, a 1932 Ford can be built with no original parts.

Seventy-five years after its introduction, the hot-rodding world is still awash in '32 Fords. There is little doubt that more 1932 Fords are registered and on the road today than Henry ever built. He must be looking down with pride at the fact that he created such a significant car, and smiling at the love and passion that people have for his creation—the amazing 1932 Ford.

CHAPTER ONE

The Fordmobile Through the Model A

Ford introduced the Model T in 1913. By the time this 1915 model was introduced, he had perfected the assembly line process of building cars. This allowed Ford to build more cars, faster, and at a lower cost than his competitors.

20 ■ DEUCE: 75 YEARS OF THE '32 FORD

In America anything is possible. Many young men from humble beginnings have grown up to be presidents. Others have worked hard and remained focused on an idea that would eventually change the world. Henry Ford was one of these men. In 1896, Ford built his first car—the Quadricycle—and seven years later was positioned to launch a motorcar company that would change history. His rise to automotive power didn't come easily. Before his ultimate success, he was involved with two failed auto companies: The Detroit Automobile Company and the Henry Ford Company.

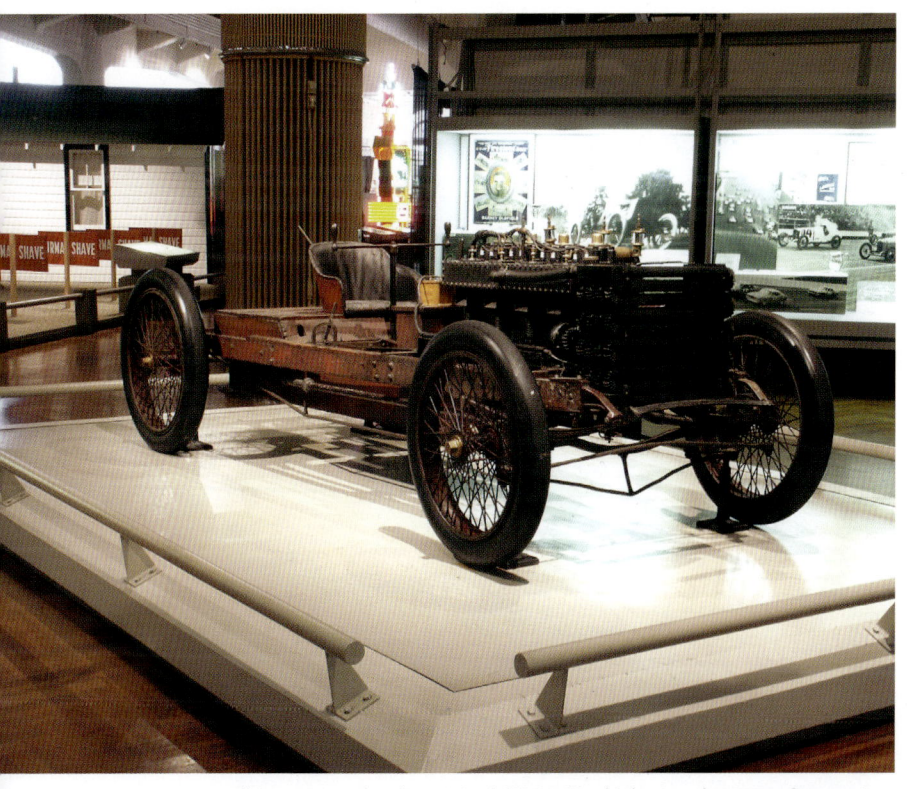

This is Henry Ford's original "'999,'" which won the Manufacturer's Challenge Cup in 1902. Built by Ford himself, the car has no body, no hood, and a wooden chassis. Ford was one of the first to realize that racing attracted customers to buy new cars.

Ford wanted the freedom to use his fertile mechanical imagination, but he needed cash. He approached Alexander Malcomson to be a partner in the new auto company. Malcomson owned Malcomson Coal Company, the firm that supplied coal to the power plants of the Edison Illuminating Company. This is where he first met Henry Ford, who was the company's chief engineer. Malcomson admired Ford for his mechanical talents and racecar driving skills. In exchange for Ford's patents, drawings, and talent as an engineer and a car builder, Malcomson agreed to fund the venture. On August 20, 1902, a partnership was formed. The first two employees were James Couzens, brought in by Malcomson from his coal company as office manager to oversee the business; and C. Harold Willis, an auto-racing friend of Ford's, recruited as his shop assistant. Malcomson provided the capital, Couzens brought the business sense, Ford offered the engineering vision, and Willis furnished the mechanical skills for construction.

At this time Henry Ford was just 39 years old. Throughout his life he had tinkered with and repaired anything mechanical that he could get his hands on. Before joining Edison Illuminating Company as a maintenance engineer, he worked in several machine shops. He quickly rose to chief engineer and built his first car on his own time, after working hours. His engineering abilities led him to build racecars and he left Edison to devote more time to auto racing. At the turn of the 20th Century, Ford's name was highly respected in Detroit for his racing and car building skills. On June 16, 1903, the Articles of Incorporation were filed for the Ford Motor Company. Now all Ford had to do was design and build a marketable car.

One of the investors offered an old wagon shop on Detroit's Mack Avenue to house the production facility. In 1903, Ford's first production car—the Model A—came into production. It was a car built primarily from off-the-shelf components. The chassis came from the Dodge Brothers, the body and seats came from the C.R. Wilson Carriage Company. The wheels were purchased from Pruddent and the tires from Hartford Rubber. The first ad for the new Fordmobile appeared in a magazine in July touting it as the "Boss of the Road," and the "most advanced auto manufactured today." Soon after the ad appeared, a check for $850, the full price of the car, arrived in the mail. By the end of the first month, 23 cars had been ordered.

Ford's Model A touring car was like most cars of the era. It looked more like a horse-drawn buggy than what we think of today as a car. And similar to the other cars of the day, the steering wheel was on the right-hand side, and there was no windshield or top. A two-cylinder, eight-horsepower gasoline engine connected to a two-speed planetary transmission propelled the vehicle. The entire rear seating section could be removed, creating a turtleback runabout.

Of the 52 car manufacturers that debuted in 1903, only Cadillac and Ford have survived to this day. Ford and Cadillac also broke into the top three in sales that year. Leading the sales list was Olds with 4,000 cars, followed by Cadillac with 2,497, and then Ford at 1,708. Total industry output for 1903 was 11,235 units.

The new Ford Motor Company was off and running, but competition was fierce with new car companies forming weekly. A new and larger factory was designed and built in Detroit at the corner of Beaubien and Piquette. Manufacturing began there in late 1904. New versions of the Ford car were tagged with letter designations. By 1906 they were up to the letter "N." Also in 1906, the relationship between the company's investors and Henry Ford and James Couzens was flagging. Ford and Couzens were doing the lion's share of the work and resented the huge dividends the investors were raking in. Initial investor Alexander Malcomson started flexing his one-quarter ownership muscle by insisting on a high-priced car. The six-cylinder Model K was built to satisfy him. This exceptionally big car didn't sell well and was soon dropped. Malcomson and a few other investors soon left and Henry Ford took control of the company. With the departure of Malcomson, Ford was now free to run the company according to his vision and to build the cars he wanted.

The Model T

The automobile was a great invention. But like all inventions, it didn't become great until it reached and benefited the masses. In recent history we've seen how the

The Model T roadster was not much more than a motorized buckboard wagon. Creature comforts were more than a decade away. Motoring was still an adventure in the era of the Model T.

Ford's Model T coupes were boxy and lacked style, but they were the least expensive and most durable coupes made. Enclosing the passenger compartment was the first step to making an all-weather car.

introductions of the cellular phone, the personal computer, and the Internet have changed the everyday lives and habits of millions of people around the world. Ford knew that his automobile could end the isolation of rural America and make travel easier than ever. By 1908 automobiles had become accepted by Americans and were no longer the playthings of the rich and famous. Also during this time, the standardization of parts and new methods of mass production continually drove down the price of each car. For Ford Motor Company, the introduction of the Model T in 1908 came at just the

When the Model T was introduced in 1908, it was the culmination of five years of work by Henry Ford and a small staff of engineers. The Model T was the latest in the series of "alphabet cars" that Ford built. The rugged Model T became a success story for the auto industry and the Ford Motor Company.

right time in American history and helped make it the car for the masses.

By 1906, Ford had moved through the alphabet from A to S. He had 1,500 employees and dealerships in most major cities. And by then the Ford name had become synonymous with affordability and durability. The success of his company was the result of a little luck, excellent management, and first-rate cars. Even with this short history of success, it would have been impossible to predict the impact of the new Model T.

Model T production started in October 1908. It was a simple but sturdy car. Its four-cylinder engine developed 20 horsepower, it featured a planetary transmission operated with a foot pedal, and it had a flywheel magneto and a prominent brass radiator. Improved manufacturing methods reduced the price of the new Model T to less than that of a new wagon and team of horses—a critical threshold. Ford sold 10,202 Model Ts in 1908.

To emphasize the durability of the new Model T, Ford entered two of them in a 1909 transcontinental race. The first competitor to cross the finish line after three tough weeks of driving was a Ford Model T. It proved to be more durable than the other cars competing and could be purchased at half the price. Sales in 1909 were 10,607 units.

During 1913 Ford implemented the assembly line for production of the Model T. While Ford historically gets credit for the invention of the assembly line, he simply adopted the method that had been used in other smaller industries since the mid-1800s. The savings were immense. Prior to the implementation of the assembly line, it took 12-1/2 man-hours to assemble a complete chassis. Now on the Ford assembly line, a Model T chassis could be built in only 1-1/2 man-hours. By 1914, Ford's Model T assembly lines were fully implemented, reducing the cost of cars and increasing their production numbers.

Ford's Highland Park plant, opened in 1910, had become the business model for manufacturing efficiency, but Henry Ford had an even larger vision. Upon 2,000 acres he had acquired in Dearborn, he built the Rouge plant, so named for the river that it was built upon. When it opened in 1927, the Rouge plant was the world's greatest industrial complex. The Rouge plant was a city within a city. With direct access to the Great Lakes and major rail lines, raw materials came in one end and cars came out the other. Today, the Rouge plant stands as one of Ford's greatest achievements and was the birthplace of millions of cars manufactured by the Ford Motor Company.

The opening of the Rouge plant coincided with the last year for the Model T. The Model T had been a phenomenal success, but the pressure of the market demanded something new. Ford ended Model T production on May 26, 1927, with a total of 15 million built since production started in 1908. Chevrolet had been nipping at the heels of Ford and would soon surpass Ford in sales. Cars were becoming a personal statement of one's individuality as much as a mode of transportation. Chevrolet was quick to add color to its cars, while Ford resisted such innovation. With the arrival of designer Harley Earl to General Motors, automotive styling would be more important than ever in customers' car buying decisions.

The Model A

On December 2, 1927, Ford unveiled its new Model A. It was estimated that ten million people saw the new

By the time the new Model As came out in 1928, Ford's massive Rouge complex was up and running. It provided Ford with the ability to build cars more efficiently than anyone else.

THE FORDMOBILE THROUGH THE MODEL A

Ford's 1929 Model A roadster was one of the many models that allowed Ford regain the sales lead. The public now demanded more attractive cars and Henry Ford had finally relented, allowing colors other than black on his Model As.

The Model A was the first Ford car that offered a rumble seat to carry two additional passengers.

This 1930 Ford represents the second generation of Ford's successful Model A series. By the end of production in 1931, Ford had sold several million of the sturdy cars. Cars of this era were also becoming more glamorous with the addition of wind wings, cowl lights, and side-mounted spare tires.

Model A in the first two days, mostly at dealerships and special displays. Ford salesmen were taking cash deposits for the new cars even though cars would not be available for weeks because of production delays. The nation yearned for a classy, low priced car; the Model A, with its proven Ford name, filled the bill.

The Model A was the most stylish Ford to date. The look came from the pen of Edsel Ford, Henry's son. Edsel had been in charge of the upscale Lincoln branch since its acquisition in 1922. With his design and marketing skills, he fostered it into one of the most prestigious marques in America. Edsel added a little of the Lincoln look to the design of the new Model A, and the buying public loved it. Color was also important to the new Model A. New paint technology allowed the wider use of colors. The new Model A was also advanced technically. Henry was heavily involved in the design of the new frame, new engine, new transmission, and innovative electrical system.

Ford regained the sales lead in 1929, but the competition stepped up with bigger engines. After several manufacturers introduced V-8s in 1928, Buick and Oldsmobile followed suit with their own V-8s. Chevrolet offered a straight six, but Ford stood fast with its four.

This Model A sedan shows how elegant the low-priced American automobile had become. The cars of the 1930s were no longer seen as luxury items for the rich, but as utilitarian vehicles for everyone.

Ford's 1930 Model A was redesigned with a taller hood, a revised cowl, and new fenders as its most prominent features. The larger hood would allow for the new V-8 engines that Ford engineers were designing in secret. However, the Great Depression was felt across the auto industry in 1930, and sales fell dramatically. Ford maintained its sales lead with 1.1 million units sold. Chevrolet was in distant second place with 640,980 units sold.

In an attempt to boost sales in 1931, Ford added three new body styles: a Town Sedan, a Victoria Coupe, and a two-door Convertible Sedan. Ford produced its 20 millionth car, a Model A Town Sedan four-door, but sales slid to a dismal 615,455 units. The final Model A Ford was built on November 1, 1931.

By 1931, Henry Ford had created an automotive and industrial legacy that was almost mythical. He created the amazing Model T and revolutionized the way the average American viewed transportation. He created the world's largest industrial complex and boosted worker's wages. Now with the country in the midst of the Great Depression—when most prudent men would either maintain the status quo or pull back—he went forward with plans to create the first low-cost V-8 engine, and to put it in a completely new car.

CHAPTER TWO

The New 1932 Ford

Even though America was in the depths of a depression, people were still interested in the new cars—especially the new V-8 Ford. This recreation of a Ford dealership, circa 1932, at the Petersen Museum recreates some of the grandeur of the dealerships of that era, where nattily dressed salesmen sat behind mahogany desks. (David Newhardt)

THE NEW 1932 FORD

In 1932, the country was in the depths of an economic depression. Many people were out of work and unable to pay for the basic needs of life, much less a new car. To make matters worse, Chevrolet overtook Ford as the sales leader in 1931, with Plymouth closing in. The automotive world was changing and Henry Ford had been resistant to many of those changes. As cars became more comfortable to drive, buyers looked for power and beauty as well as utility. The desire for horsepower was addressed with the addition of a new V-8, but it would take a completely restyled car to attract the buying public. Ford wanted to regain and maintain the level of automotive sales leadership he had grown to enjoy. He knew he had to offer an all-new car for 1932. The new model should be good looking and include features never before offered in a Ford. And most importantly, the new '32 would be affordable.

Ford offered 10 body styles with 14 different models in 1932. Engineers designed this new model to be a dramatic departure from the Model A. Its silhouette was lower and more streamlined. Ford eliminated the bulky visor and leaned the windshield back at a rakish 10 degrees. A dramatic grille shell covered the radiator and offered an attractive grille in a V shape with vertical bars. Ford set a new standard of performance and style with the new 1932 Ford.

Ford only produced 282,797 Fords domestically in 1932. In the 75 years since that time, cars were scrapped by the thousands to make battleships and tanks for World War II, and, following the war, jalopy racers used old Ford sedans like a cold sufferer uses Kleenex. Yet people still keep finding original '32s in barns and garages.

The Body

Early automobile coachbuilders were accustomed to working in wood and most of the early automobiles contained a great deal of wooden structure. As the craft progressed and coachbuilders learned how to work with steel, less and less wood was used. In the 1920s, the art of engineering an automobile body developed along with advanced techniques for metal forming and welding. Late in 1931, Ford introduced its first all-steel body shell in the form of a simple commercial pickup truck. The natural progression of this advancement in coach building would be reflected in the new 1932 Ford; its body, exterior panels, and interior structure were made mostly from steel. It took more than five years for Chevrolet to follow suit. Ford used wood for the mounting structure of the quarter window regulators in the convertible sedan and Victoria. Ford also used wood in all the bod-

Ford built its 1932 models with all-steel construction. Previously, wood had been used extensively throughout the body. This all-steel construction is one of the reasons so many '32 Fords have survived.

This 1932 Ford display features a complete V-8 chassis. Many of the components were chrome plated while others were cut away to show spectators the car's inner workings.

THE NEW 1932 FORD

Maggini Motor Car Company has just received a shipment of new 1932 Fords. A pair of V-8 equipped two-door sedans flank a V-8 Phaeton. The hood on the Phaeton has been removed and the engine compartment wrapped in clear plastic so the customers can see the new V-8 engine.

Ford offered 14 models for 1932, including a Deluxe three-window coupe. Nothing on this body was interchangeable with any of the 1932 models. It was the first Ford to offer suicide, or rear-hinged, doors.

ies for tack strips. Wood was also used for structure in some of the lower production bodies such as the Sport Coupe and Sedan Delivery.

The car-buying public was used to open cars and Ford continued to build and sell Roadsters and Phaetons, even though closed cars were much more practical. As automobile construction improved, allowing enclosed seating compartments that provided greater comfort for passengers, open cars with side curtains became less desirable. Yet some segments of the market—particularly people living in warm climates—continued to buy open cars. The Roadster was also Ford's least expensive model.

The fact that Ford offered so many body styles was most puzzling, particularly in light of the ongoing depression. Were two coupes really necessary? Was a convertible sedan necessary? Ford produced an excessive number of body styles in 1932 with very little, or no, interchangeability between models. Although such diversity provided a car for every customer's taste, it also drove up production costs. The Ford Motor Company might have been more profitable in 1932 had it limited the number of body styles and increased the interchangeability between models.

The chassis components of the 1932 Ford that were designed to be interchangeable between all models included the firewall, the hood, and the fenders (three different sets of rear fenders), along with some minor frame rail covers. These components, and the gas tank, were also all painted black, and painted separately from the body. Ford used a process called "Bonderizing" on the fenders, front splash shield, front spreader bar, front

The fenders on all 1932 Fords were painted with black enamel. Prior to painting they were treated with a process called "Bonderizing," which prevented rust from spreading if the paint were scratched.

CHAPTER TWO

license plate bracket, rear fender aprons, spare wheel assembly, and taillight brackets. This Bonderizing treatment of the bare metal prepared it for the enamel and provided a minimal rust barrier. All of these components were painted with black enamel. They also used the Bonderizing process on the wheels, which Ford painted black and several other colors.

Ford designers created fenders with graceful curves on the new 1932 model. They preserved the basic design of the Model A's fenders, but the new 1932 Ford fenders were less angular. The smooth, sweeping design of the fenders was very reminiscent of the fender design on the Lincoln model. Ford created three sets of rear fenders for the passenger car: a wide one for the Coupes and Roadsters, another for the Sedans including the Victoria, and a third set for the Convertible Sedan.

There were also two different front fender designs, one of which featured a spare tire well. Because of design constraints, certain models such as the station wagon, pickup truck, and sedan delivery could not use a rear-mounted spare tire. Ford created a spare tire well in the front fender for these models and the customer could select a right or left spare tire. The side-mounted spare could be added to any other 1932 Ford body style except

Both the front and rear fenders on all 1932 Fords were a one-piece design. Ford rolled a wire into the outer exposed edges for a smoother rounded edge.

32 ■ DEUCE: 75 YEARS OF THE '32 FORD

Phaetons, such as this Deluxe model, and Roadsters did not offer any type of locking mechanism for the doors. The only security system the owner of a Roadster or Phaeton had was the locking steering column.

Ford offered two different front fenders for its 1932 models. One was plain and a second was made with a well for a spare tire. Because of their construction, certain models—such as the pickup trucks (roadster and closed), panel truck, and sedan delivery—required the side-mounted spare. Because of its door swing, the three-window coupe was the only model that could not be fitted with a side-mounted spare.

A close inspection of the lower left corner of this 1932 Ford roadster's wind wing reveals the Ford logo and date of manufacture, August 1932. This original piece of Ford safety glass is starting to delaminate around the edges.

33 ■ DEUCE: 75 YEARS OF THE '32 FORD

Basic 1932 Ford Chassis Specifications

Construction	Body on frame
Wheelbase	106 inches
Frame rails	Stamped steel
Frame rail length	148.375 inches
Frame rail height	6 inches
Frame rail width	2 inches
Crossmembers	three riveted in place, two bolted in at the ends of the frame
Fuel tank	14 gallons
Wheels	18-inch diameter drop center with 32 spokes
Tires	18 x 5.25 black wall
Hood	Length 32 inches (20 or 25 louvers)
Tread	Front 55 inches, Rear 56.28 inches
Turning radius	19 feet 6 inches
Transmission	3-speed constant mesh, 1st 2.82:1, 2nd 1.60:1, 3rd 1:1
Steering gear	Worm and sector 13:1 ratio
Road clearance	8.25-inches
Springs	Transverse leaf front and rear
Rear axle	Three-quarter floating 4.11:1 ratio
Front axle	I-beam forging
Shock absorbers	Houdaille hydraulic double acting
Headlights	9.25 diameter, 21 candle power
Battery	Located under driver's floor
Electrical system	Positive ground, 6 volts
Brakes	Mechanical four-wheel, internal expanding shoe
Emergency brake	Hand operated (activates all four wheels)
Radiator	Tube & fin, 374 square inches

the three-window Deluxe Coupe; its longer rear-hinged door could not swing past the tire. The side-mounted spare tire included a sturdy bracket that attached to the side of the car's cowl and the frame. Customers who wanted the ultimate upscale automotive look in 1932 could opt for dual side mounts.

The 1932 Ford grille shell is exceptionally distinctive and utterly beautiful. Like so many other components of the 1932 Ford, the grille shell's design heritage comes from the 1931 and 1932 Lincoln. The Model A's grille shell was no more than an extension of the radiator—a rectangular object with sharp corners. For 1932, Ford designers shaped a grille shell similar to that of the high-end Duesenberg or Cord, with a smoothly rounded nose and a pronounced "V" shape to the grille insert. This design was a dramatic departure from the low-priced cars of the era that still featured grille shells like those of the Model A. Ford painted the V-shaped insert Sea Gull Gray on its entire line of passenger cars. The grille shell on the commercial models looked similar to the passenger car's grille, but the vertical bars were formed by the stamped openings instead of a separate grille insert. Ford painted the shell on these commercial vehicles the color of the body and painted the grille bars black. In July 1932, Ford painted the vertical bars black on those commercial vehicles that were painted either Vermillion or Golden Orange. Those painted Mountain Blue, Blue Rock Green or white were painted the same color as the body.

Because of the vertical grille shell and vertical cowl, there wasn't much Ford designers could do with the

THE NEW 1932 FORD

The hood on the 1932 Ford was constructed of four hinged panels. Early production cars were fitted with hoods that had 20 vertical louvers per side. Later in the production cycle, Ford increased the number of louvers to 25. The hood on this Deluxe four-door sedan has 20 louvers.

CHAPTER TWO

Ford painted the vertical bars on its 1932 Ford grille Sea Gull Gray. This was the first year Ford offered a separate grille insert on its passenger cars.

1932 Ford hood that would make it unique. Like all four-piece car hoods of the era, it featured a center hinge and hinged side panels. Over the model year on the passenger cars, the only variances were in the side panels and latches. Initially, each hood side was constructed with 20 vertical louvers; in September of that year, Ford increased the number to 25 to better cool the engine. Ford also changed the hood latches early in the production cycle from an "L"-shaped latch to the "T" style.

One of the most highly identifiable features of the 1932 Ford, when compared to the Model A, is the 10-degree rake of the windshield. This design element, called streamlining, is found in the art deco movement and is seen in the design of buildings and trains of the era. Ford's designers must have been influenced

The A-pillars on the 1932 Ford were leaned back at 10 degrees. This was Ford's first attempt at streamlining its designs. Ford also hinged the windshield at the top so it could be opened for additional ventilation. The windshield frame on this Victoria should be painted body color. The only closed car with a chrome windshield frame was the three-window coupe.

36 ■ DEUCE: 75 YEARS OF THE '32 FORD

Standard & Deluxe

In the early 1930s, as low-priced cars were becoming more than a means of transportation, buyers were looking for improved content. Henry Ford's old-school thinking of painting all cars black quickly fell out of favor in the late 1920s. In the early 1930s, cars were becoming a fashion statement and colors were a requirement. While black still topped the list of available colors for the 1932 Ford automobiles, many two-tone paint combinations were available, even as an option on Standard models. In addition, The Ford Motor Company offered a Standard and Deluxe version of nearly every model it produced in 1932. The exceptions were the three-window coupe, which was only sold in the Deluxe trim, and the five-window coupe that Ford offered strictly as a Standard model with no Deluxe version. The Victoria Sedan, the Convertible Sedan (B-400) and Cabriolet were not advertised as Deluxe or Standard models, but featured many of the Deluxe model upgrades such as Tapestry carpeting, safety glass, and cowl lamps.

Ford's Deluxe versions offered the buyer a higher level of interior trim with a few select extras that made motoring more elegant. The most easily identified component of a Deluxe model 1932 Ford was the cowl lights. These small lights were attached to the cowl side and provided a parking light function on the Deluxe models. These lights could be bought at any Ford dealer's parts counter and easily installed on any Standard model. Ford engineers had the foresight to include the inner cowl reinforcements to all 1932 Ford bodies.

All frames and fenders were painted black, but Ford's 1932 Deluxe models were painted in seven attractive two-tone color combinations (solid black was also available). Ford fitted all Standard models with black wheels. All Deluxe cars came with wheels colorfully painted in Tacoma Cream, Apple Green, or Aurora Red. On special order, the wheels on a Standard could be painted these colors. Deluxe buyers could also opt for black wheels.

The biggest differences between a 1932 Ford Standard and Deluxe model were seen in the interior appointments. Standard models used several types of basic, durable materials for the seats and door trim panels. The Deluxe models used much richer materials for the interior trim, including real leather for the seating surfaces on some models. Deluxe models also featured wood-grained instrument panels and window frames, while Ford painted the Standard model's instrument panel and window frames interior gray. Ford also fitted all of its Deluxe models with Tapestry carpeting, rear seat ashtrays, and windows with laminated glass (all 1932 Fords were equipped with a laminated windshield). Ford also offered laminated glass as an option on Standard models, but the carpeting had to be installed at the dealer.

Offering two distinctly different levels of trim was a first for Ford. It is still a tradition in the automotive industry today.

by this design trend. In addition to creating this rearward lean of the windshield, designers removed the sunshade from the header. This would be the first Ford passenger car fitted with interior fold-down sun visors. The removal of the exterior sunshade cleaned up the design substantially. Another feature on the new '32 Ford closed car, setting it apart from the Model A, was the radiused upper corners of the windshield frame. The Cabriolet, Sport Coupe, Convertible Sedan, Station Wagon, and all commercial vehicles used a windshield frame similar to the mitered upper corners of the Model A.

The Chassis

The frame design for the 1932 Ford was a "ladder" design similar to the one used on the Model A. It featured two large side rails connected by smaller "rungs" that resembled a ladder. However, the side rails designed for 1932 used a considerably larger section than those used on the Model A. At its widest point the 1932 Ford rail measured six inches high with a depth of 2 inches. There were five crossmember components on the '32 Ford frame. The front and rear, which are commonly called "spreader bars," offered a small amount of structural

CHAPTER TWO

The front spreader bar on the 1932 Ford's frame incorporated the front license plate bracket and a support for the hand engine crank.

stability to the assembly. Bolts attached the front and rear spreader bars to the frame rail at each respective end. The front bar doubled as a front license plate mount and the stabilizing point for the engine crank handle. There were several types of rear spreader bars; the most common one mounted the rear spare tire. The other three crossmembers were permanently riveted to the frame rails. The front crossmember was located 14 inches behind the front spreader bar. This large inverted "U" shaped section provided the mount for the front spring, front engine mounts, and radiator attachment points. There were two different front crossmembers prior to May 1932: one that mounted a V-8 engine and one that mounted a four-cylinder engine. After that date, engineers added a new front crossmember that accepted the motor mounts of both engines.

The largest crossmember on the 1932 Ford frame was a "K"-shaped assembly of stampings that served as the rear mount for the engine/transmission and also the rear-most mount for the front suspension radius rod assembly. The engine/transmission mount used a rubber ring to isolate vibration. In 1932, Ford would use rubber isolators extensively to reduce component vibration. The rear crossmember was a large "U"-shaped section that provided the mount for the rear spring. Previously on the Model A, the rear spring was mounted directly over the axle. In 1932, engineers moved the rear spring behind the rear axle to obtain better ride quality and create a lower center of gravity. The lack of strength and rigidity in the frame was a constant challenge for Ford engineers throughout the production year. The weight of the rear-mounted spare and fuel tank created a problem in the area over the rear axle. In many cases this area of the frame rail became distorted. Ford addressed this problem with the addition of a riveted reinforcement to the outside of the frame rail and then later in production with a welded-in reinforcement.

The problem with any ladder frame is that it lacks torsion stability. The side rails move forward and back in an independent but parallel fashion, pivoting on the attachment points on each rung. The car is said to "matchbox." In 1933, Ford changed the frame design to include a large "X"-style crossmember that increased the overall rigidity of the frame, because it prevented the matchbox effect.

Ford designed a new chassis for the 1932 Ford. The frame rails were larger and stronger than those used on the Model A. One unusual feature of the 1932 Ford is its exposed frame rail. Ford enhanced the design by adding a character line where the frame meets the fenders and running board.

38 ■ DEUCE: 75 YEARS OF THE '32 FORD

THE NEW 1932 FORD

The chrome bumpers Ford added to each of its cars in 1932 were of a ribbed design and were advertised to prevent the bumpers of another car from riding over or under in a minor accident. To lower the base price of the car, Ford listed the bumpers as a required option on all cars.

Ford chassis engineers mounted Houdaille friction shocks at all four corners of the 1932 Ford frame. Cars equipped with a V-8 featured an automatic temperature-sensing control that maintained the shock absorber's adjustment in cold or hot weather. These self-adjusting shocks were added to the four-cylinder equipped cars in April 1932, replacing the manual adjustment-style shocks Ford had been installing. Later in the model year, other minor shock absorber changes were made to specific models to further improve the ride.

Mounted at the front and rear of the frame were a pair of identical bumpers. These chrome-plated bumpers featured a corrugated sectional shape with curled ends. Although they were installed on all 1932 Fords, the bumpers were listed as an option. This little marketing trick allowed Ford to advertise a lower list price for the car.

The most interesting aspect of the 1932 Ford frame was its exposed side rail above the running board. By contrast, the Model A's frame was small and covered by a curved panel that extended from the bottom of the body to the running board. For 1932, Ford engineers did away with the covers and added a character line (often called a "beauty mark") to the side of the rail. This line followed the shape of the running board and swept up

39 ■ DEUCE: 75 YEARS OF THE '32 FORD

CHAPTER TWO

The Colorful 1932 Fords

Urban legend has it that when Henry Ford released the Model T there was only one color for him—black. The truth is that between 1908 and 1913 there were Model Ts in several different colors. But the colored cars took much longer for the paint to cure, slowing down production; thus, Ford made a lot of black cars. Consumers liked color and Ford relented by adding several attractive colors to the Model As. For 1932, color would also be part of his new line of cars. Black would be Ford's primary color and the set color of all 1932 Standard models, and an optional color on Deluxe models. When black was specified on a Deluxe model, the suggested color for the wheels was Apple Green; however, the owner had the freedom to choose any color wheel. The pinstripes on Ford's 1932 black cars were gold. Here's how all of the colors broke down for 1932.

Body, Hood, & Grille Shell	Body Moldings	Pin Stripe	Wheels (suggested color)
Washington Blue	Black	Tacoma Cream	Tacoma Cream
Old Chester Gray	Tunis Gray	Tacoma Cream	Tacoma Cream
Tunis Gray	Old Chester Gray	Tacoma Cream	Tacoma Cream
Emperor Brown Lt.	Emperor Brown Dk.	Tacoma Cream	Tacoma Cream
Winterleaf Brown Dk.	Winterleaf Brown Lt.	Tacoma Cream	Tacoma Cream
Brewster Green Med.	Brewster Green Lt.	Silver Gray	Apple Green
Brewster Green Med.	Brewster Green Lt. (includes upper body)	Silver Gray	Apple Green
Ford Med. Maroon	Black	Gold	Aurora Red
Black	Black	Gold	Apple Green

along the top edge of the rear portion of the front fender. In addition to its aesthetic value, this slight depression added to the strength of the rail. This exposed frame rail elegantly tied the body, fenders, and running board together. This would be the only year that Ford would use an exposed frame rail.

The left frame rail was also where the vehicle identification number was stamped on all 1932 Fords. When the engines were installed (V-8 or four cylinder), the vehicle identification number was stamped on the engine's flywheel cover and onto the top of the left frame rail in front of the firewall attaching points. All 1932 Ford serial numbers were proceeded by and followed by an asterisk (*). This serial number would also be stamped in the area of the driver's door and over the rear axle; however, only the one forward of the firewall was visible once the car was assembled.

The suspension on the '32 Ford was similar to that of the Model A. It featured transverse springs, a beam front axle, and a solid rear axle. The front axle used an

This is the front right tire of a 1932 Ford. Ford's forged I-beam axle was exceptionally strong and featured an arched center. The drum brakes on all 1932 Fords were mechanically actuated. The brake actuating rod is connected to the rod extending from the upper portion of the backing plate.

40 ■ DEUCE: 75 YEARS OF THE '32 FORD

Ford used a wooden framework to support the fixed roof insert on its sedan and coupe models. All of the top inserts were black vinyl.

CHAPTER TWO

The low profile of this Ford roadster is due to the advanced chassis that Ford engineers designed for 1932. To lower the center of gravity, they moved the rear spring behind the rear axle. On Model As, the rear spring was directly over the axle.

I-beam section that was much larger than the Model A's axle and had a much deeper arch in the center. The spindles were new but the tie rod assembly was carried over from the Model A. The 1932 Ford rear axle was a 3/4 floating design with a torque tube drive. Ford engineers mounted the spring behind the axle for a smoother ride; this method allowed for a lower ride height. Upon initial production, Ford used two different rear axle ratios: a 3.78:1 for the four-cylinder engine and a 4.33:1 for the V-8 equipped cars, later

Here a Ford salesman is demonstrating a new B-400's turning capability by doing repeated donuts around a post. The turning radius of a new 1932 Ford was 19 feet.

42 ■ DEUCE: 75 YEARS OF THE '32 FORD

THE NEW 1932 FORD

For 1932, Ford removed the visor from the header and added interior sun visors for both the driver and passenger. Ford only offered one steering wheel. It was a three-spoke design with a 17-inch diameter rim.

changing to 4.11:1 gear ratio for all engines. Late in the 1932 production cycle, Ford introduced a revised axle design. During the 1932 Ford's production cycle, two different front springs were used, both having 12 leaves. Five different rear springs were used depending on body style: two of the springs had 9 leaves, one had 10, one 11, and the one used on the commercial chassis had 13 leaves.

Henry Ford insisted on mechanical brakes on the 1932 Ford. With minor modifications, Ford would continue to use mechanical brakes through the 1938 model year. The 1932 Ford's chrome parking brake handle was also carried over from the Model A and when pulled, activated the brakes on all four wheels.

The 1932 Ford rode on spoked steel wheels that were 18 inches in diameter. The rim was 3.25 inches wide and was laced with 32 spokes. Wheels on a Standard model were black, but buyers could order wheels painted any of the brighter colors offered as standard equipment on the Deluxe models. The only tire available from the factory

Ford only offered one tire size from the factory: a 5-1/4 x 18 black sidewall. White sidewall tires were available as a dealer installed option only. This would be the only year that Ford fitted its cars with 18-inch diameter wheels. The trim rings on these wheels are also a dealer accessory option.

43 ■ DEUCE: 75 YEARS OF THE '32 FORD

CHAPTER TWO

All new 1932 Fords rolled on a new 106-inch wheelbase. Also new for Ford in 1932 were 32-spoke, 18-inch diameter wheels. This is a five-window coupe, one of two different coupe models offered by Ford in 1932.

The wheels on Ford's 1932 Deluxe models, such as this Victoria sedan, were offered in a variety of colors, in this case Apple Green, or black.

44 ■ DEUCE: 75 YEARS OF THE '32 FORD

THE NEW 1932 FORD

Ford offered two different hubcaps on its 1932 models. This hubcap with the Ford oval logo was used on the cars equipped with the four-cylinder engine. The V-8 equipped models were fitted with a similar hubcap with a V-8 logo in the center instead of the Ford oval.

in 1932 was a 5.25 x 18 blackwall. Whitewall tires were offered as an option or at the dealers. At the beginning of the model year the new 1932 Ford was only equipped with four tires because of a limited supply of 5.25 x 18 tires. The wheel for the spare was included, but the tire was added later at the delivering dealership. This was the only year 18-inch tires were offered as standard equipment on a Ford. In 1933, Ford went to 17-inch wheels and in 1935, to 16-inch wheels.

Ford offered two hubcaps for the 1932 Ford and both were the same 6.75-inch diameter made from stainless steel. The V-8 equipped cars had a "V-8" embossed into the center of the hubcap and those with the four-cylinder engine had a Ford script within an oval stamped in the center. The backgrounds on both the logos were painted in Harding Blue.

On the Model A the gas tank was in the cowl, directly in front of the passenger compartment. While this location provided a direct supply of gravity fed gasoline to the engine, it also was a source of gas fumes to the car's occupants. For 1932, Ford relocated the gas tank on its passenger cars to the rear of the frame between the rear crossmember and the rear spreader bar. All of these rear-mounted tanks had a capacity of 14 gallons. Commercial body styles used a tank located under the driver's seat.

For 1932 Ford moved the gas tank from the cowl, where it was on the Model A, to the rear of the car. All of these rear-mounted tanks had a 14-gallon capacity. Most 1932 Ford commercial vehicles, with the exception of this Sedan Delivery, had the gas tank mounted under the front passenger seat. Also of interest on this Sedan Delivery is the straight rear spreader bar, used on vehicles with side-mounted spare tires.

45 ■ DEUCE: 75 YEARS OF THE '32 FORD

CHAPTER TWO

Instrumentation and Controls

The center of the instrument panel on all 1932 Fords featured an oval-shaped insert that mounted three gauges. On all V-8 equipped cars, this insert was chrome-plated with an engine-turned finish. Initially, commercial vehicles and passenger cars with a four-cylinder engine used a painted insert.

In the center of the panel, engineers mounted a speedometer that read a maximum of 80 miles per hour. In May 1932, Ford changed to a 90 mile-per-hour

Ford initially offered only one speedometer that read up to 80 miles per hour. After May 1932, the V-8 equipped cars were given 90-mile-per-hour speedometers. Stewart Warner, Delco, and Waltham supplied the cable-driven speedometers to Ford. This car is also equipped with the optional temperature gauge that's incorporated into the fuel gauge.

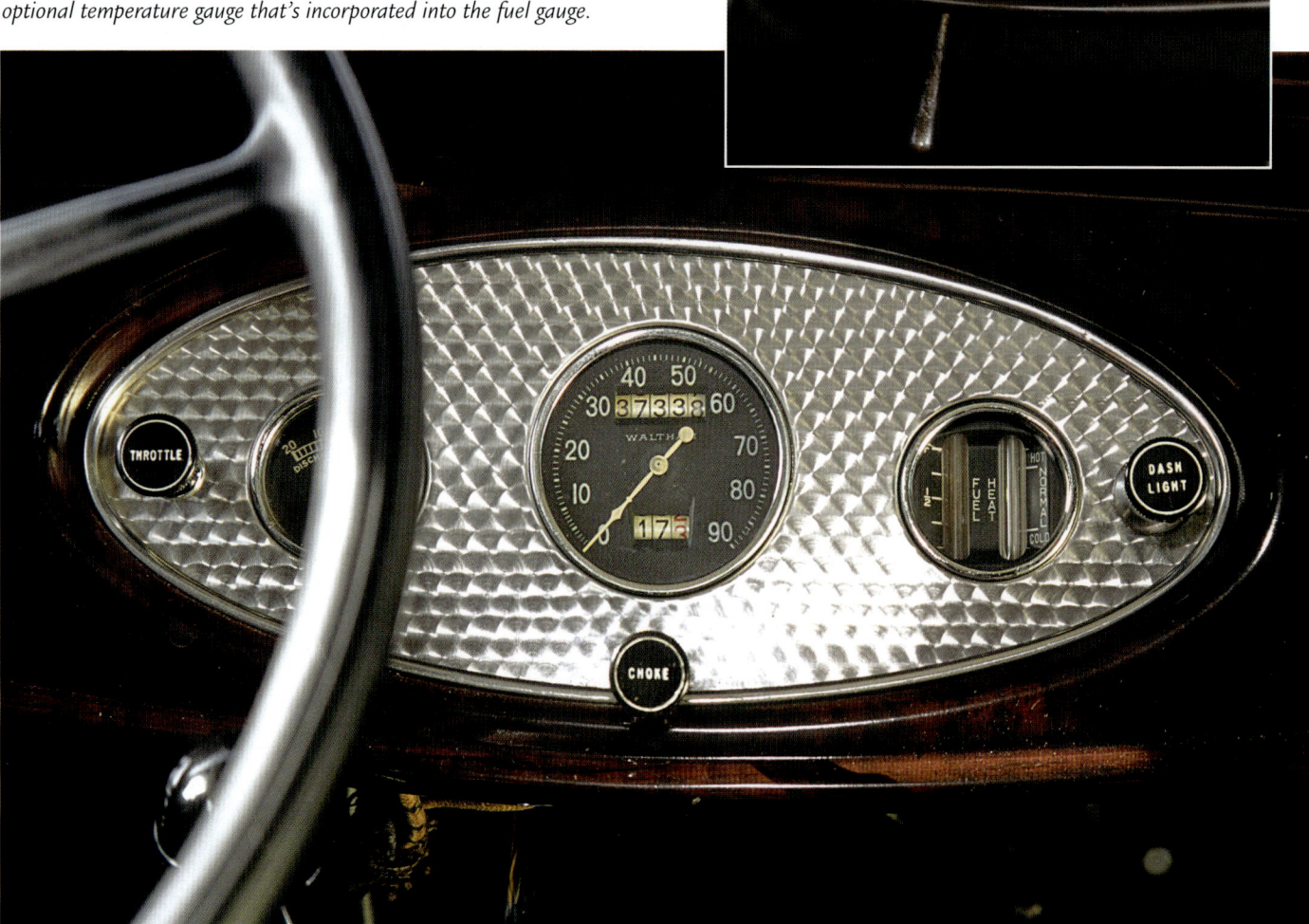

Ford mounted an engine-turned gauge panel in the center of its 1932 Ford instrument panel. Initially only the V-8 equipped cars were given the engine-turned panel, but by May 1932, all vehicles, four-cylinder and V-8, were fitted with this attractive panel.

THE NEW 1932 FORD

Ford installed its ignition lock at the base of the steering column on its 1932 Fords. In addition to switching the ignition on and off, it was also an anti-theft feature that locked the steering column, preventing the wheels from turning without the key. The longer lever protruding out of the floor on this original five-window coupe is the gearshift and the shorter one is the emergency brake.

speedometer on the V-8 equipped models. And once the supply of 80 mile-per-hour speedometers was used up, all cars were fitted with the 90 mile-per-hour model. Stewart Warner, Delco, or Waltham supplied the cable-driven speedometers Ford used throughout the 1932 production year.

On either side of the speedometer were the small fuel gauge and ammeter. The fuel gauge was mounted on the right-hand side of the instrument panel and displayed a red fluid in a vertical tube to indicate the car's fuel level. This red fluid was driven by air pressure created by the level of fuel in the tank. The pressure created by a full tank of gas caused pressure in the tube and elevated the red fluid in the gauge. As the level of fuel dropped in the tank, so did the air pressure to the gauge, resulting in a drop in the gauge's red fluid. The problem Ford had with this style of gauge was the accumulation of dirt in the air line from the tank. This would often give unreliable fuel level readings. The simple fix was to blow out the line leading to the tank. The ammeter was located on the left side of the instrument panel. It had a needle that swept from 20 to 0 to 20 with the words "discharge" and "charge" in white letters on a black background.

Late in the model year Ford also sold a combination fuel and water temperature gauge as an accessory. This unit mounted in the instrument panel opening designated for the fuel gauge. This gauge contained two vertical tubes with red fluid: the tube on the right indicated the amount of fuel in the tank, and the tube on the left indicated the engine's water temperature. The sending unit for the temperature gauge required a hole to be cut in the upper radiator hose. This gauge could be installed on the V-8 or the four-cylinder engine.

There were other controls located on the 1932 Ford V-8 instrument panel. Three pull-type phenolic knobs were located at the 3, 6, and 9 o'clock positions. These controls were for the instrument panel

47 ■ DEUCE: 75 YEARS OF THE '32 FORD

1932 Ford Domestic Production

Model	V-8	Four	Total
Phaeton	600	612	1,212
Deluxe Phaeton	978	300	1,278
Roadster	568	984	1,552
Deluxe Roadster	7,318	3,727	11,045
Standard Coupe	31,112	20,682	51,794
Sport Coupe	2,169	742	2,911
Two-door Sedan	62,697	37,122	99,819
Deluxe Two-door Sedan	20,200	4,082	24,282
Cabriolet	6,062	429	6,491
Station Wagon	331	1,052	1,383
Four-door Sedan	9,984	4,224	14,208
Deluxe Four-door Sedan	20,471	2,684	23,155
Victoria	8,054	526	8,580
Convertible Sedan	884	42	926
Deluxe Coupe	21,178	970	22,148
Sedan Delivery	58	342	400
Panel Delivery	46	3,457	3,503
Deluxe Panel Delivery	69	2,550	2,619

lights (right), choke (lower), and throttle (left). The layout on early Model Bs (four-cylinder models) had the throttle on the left and the choke on the right with no instrument panel light control. After June 1932, Ford standardized the instrument panel to the V-8 style on all models.

Located on the center of the 1932 Ford's 17-inch diameter steering wheel were the horn button and a lever-style switch for the headlights. On the 1932 Ford's steering column support, Ford engineers added an antitheft device that locked the steering. With the key in the full counterclockwise position, a spring-loaded bolt engaged a slot on the steering shaft. This locked the front wheels in position. The "on-off" ignition switch was also located on the column support next to the key. The starter button on all V-8s was located on the floor between the clutch and brake pedals. Most of the four-cylinder '32 Fords were equipped with a pull-to-start cable that was mounted on the left side of the steering

The round fixture to the right of the spoon-shaped accelerator pedal is a "dead pedal" that's used as a footrest. The small silver-colored button between the brake and clutch is the starter button.

column. A late production change added the foot-controlled starter button to these B-models.

By 1932, foot controls had been standardized within the automotive industry, placing the clutch on the left, the brake in the middle, and the accelerator pedal on the right. This was the layout for the new Ford as well. The 1932 Ford's three-speed transmission featured new helical gears and a synchronizing feature that meant a quieter transmission and smoother shifts. It used a floor shift similar to the one used on the Model A with a shift pattern in the form of the letter H.

Ford used two different transmissions in 1932: one for the four-cylinder engine and another for the V-8. Internally they were the same; the differences were in the clutch and transmission cases. Throughout the model year, Ford made several changes to the transmission. The first change happened in March 1932, when the gearshift lever was offset to the left by 2 inches. This was done to allow the lever to be in high gear when the passenger seat on the two-door and Victoria sedans was folded forward. Later in the year the lever was angled slightly to the rear to provide extra clearance to the choke knob when the transmission was in second gear.

To the right of the shift lever on the floor was the chrome parking/emergency brake handle. This hand-operated brake was connected to the mechanical brake system and actuated the brakes on all four wheels.

Electrical

All 1932 Ford vehicles used a 6-volt positive ground electrical system. Ford engineers located the battery below the driver's floor. Ford mounted the 12-amp generator on top of the V-8 and on the left side of the four-cylinder engine. Today, a 12-amp generator could not keep up with the electrical demands of a modern car, but in 1932, the electrical systems were simple, offering no high-powered options.

The 1932 Ford would be the last passenger car Ford would produce with a headlight bar. This support bar stretched in a graceful arc from fender to fender. The area of the bar between the lights on all passenger cars was wrapped with a stainless steel sleeve (commercial cars and trucks were painted black). On the cars equipped with a V-8, Ford fitted a smart looking V-8 emblem at the top center of the bar. The headlights Ford used in 1932 model were similar to the "two light" design used on the Model A. In that con-

Ford only offered one generator for its 1932 Fords. It had a total output of 12 amps—miniscule by today's automotive standards, but plenty adequate for 1932's electrical needs.

figuration, two bulbs were used inside a single headlight assembly: one for a parking light and the other for the headlight. Only Standard models were equipped with this style of light. The Deluxe model used a single bulb headlight with the cowl light functioning as a parking light. Ford designers wrapped the exterior of the headlights in a smoothly rounded stainless steel housing. Cowl lights came standard as part of the Deluxe package, but they could be easily added to

Continued on page 52

CHAPTER TWO

1932 Ford Vehicle Weights (in pounds)

Model	V-8	Four
Roadster	2,242	2,131
Deluxe Roadster	2,296	2,154
Phaeton	2,369	2,251
Deluxe Phaeton	2,375	2,268
Standard Coupe	2,382	2,261
Sport Coupe	2,396	2,286
Cabriolet	2,398	2,295
Deluxe Coupe	2,464	2,364
Two-door Sedan	2,447	2,357
Deluxe Two-door sedan	2,482	2,352
Four-door Sedan	2,425	2,398
Deluxe Four-door sedan	2,521	2,432
Victoria	2,460	2,344
Convertible Sedan	2,480	2,349

Two different headlights were used on 1932 Fords: one for the Standard model that incorporated two bulbs (one for the headlight and one for the parking light), and one for the Deluxe model that only used a single bulb for the headlights. All Deluxe models were equipped with cowl lights that functioned as parking lights. Ford used a 6-volt positive ground electrical system.

DEUCE: 75 YEARS OF THE '32 FORD

The headlight buckets on all 1932 Ford passenger cars were polished stainless steel. The wiring from the light to the grille shell ran inside a flexible stainless housing.

CHAPTER TWO

Cowl lights were a standard part of the 1932 Ford Deluxe package. Ford wisely added an inner cowl reinforcement to all bodies so anyone buying a Standard model could easily add these attractive lights.

Ford added this stylish emblem to the center of the light bar of the V-8 equipped 1932 Fords. Its design has become an icon for Ford V-8 cars.

any Standard model because Ford had added a reinforcement to the inner cowl on all cars.

Ford fitted each of its new 1932 models with a single left hand taillight that doubled as a license plate bracket. This light also had a small clear lens on the top that illuminated the license plate. An optional right hand taillight was available. Ford made the housings on passenger cars out of stainless steel, while the ones used on commercial vehicles were painted black.

The 1932 Ford's lineage to the Model A was apparent, but the new model really was a completely new car. The fact that the '32 was to last but one year was most unusual. The cost of designing and engineering a new car is usually amortized over several model years. Not so with the 1932 Ford. An entirely new model was in showrooms by 1933.

In 1932, General Motors announced that it would change its cars every year. Henry Ford reacted by creating

THE NEW 1932 FORD

A majority of the Fords produced in 1932 were equipped with the rear-mounted spare tire. The bracket that held the tire attached to the ends of the frame rails. The black circular object on the right side of the frame is a step to aid rumble seat passengers with entry and exit.

Ford mounted its 7-inch diameter headlights on an attractive headlight bar that stretched from fender to fender. The portion between the headlights was wrapped with a stainless steel sleeve except on the commercial models.

53 ■ DEUCE: 75 YEARS OF THE '32 FORD

CHAPTER TWO

Ford equipped each of its 1932 Ford passenger cars with a left-hand taillight that combined with a license plate mounting bracket. A similar right-hand light was a dealer-installed accessory.

an entirely new model for 1933. The styling of Ford's new passenger cars for 1933 was exceptionally dramatic. Ford designers laid the grille back, sweetened the lines of the body, and stretched the wheelbase. More body styles were fitted with stylish and dramatic suicide doors and the fenders were partially skirted. Ford engineers redesigned the chassis with a large X-member in the center, giving it the torsion rigidity the 1932 frame lacked. The V-8's teething problems were almost over by

The roofs on all of Ford's closed 1932 models were fitted with a black insert covering the opening in the roof. Metal stamping technology was still in its infancy in 1932, and it would be a few years before a full steel roof would be found on a Ford passenger car.

THE NEW 1932 FORD

When Ford released its 1933 Ford it was new from bumper to bumper. Ford designers slanted the grille back and streamlined the entire car. To be completely correct, the fenders on this 1933 coupe should be black.

1933 and the public realized that the V-8 engine was here to stay.

It may have lasted only one year, but the legacy of the 1932 Ford remains. Even though Chevrolet outsold it at the time, the Ford remains as the most significant car built in 1932. Its low-cost V-8 revolutionized the automobile industry and Ford's all-steel body structure was years ahead of the competition. The all-steel body is one reason that so many 1932 Fords have survived for 75 years. The other is that the design struck a chord within so many people. The adaptability of later Ford components and the hot rodding world's enthusiasm for the flathead made it an easy car to hop up. The 1932 Ford is simply *one of those cars*. The 1932 Ford exemplifies hot rodding just as the finned 1957 Chevrolet represents the 1950s. There's a reason that it's the only car built in 1932 to be nicknamed "The Deuce."

55 ■ DEUCE: 75 YEARS OF THE '32 FORD

CHAPTER THREE

The New V-8

When customers opened the hood of a new 1932 Ford, they saw the first low-cost V-8 engine ever produced. Prior to 1932 there were very few cars with V-8 engines. Those that did have V-8s were much more expensive than the new Ford.

56 ■ DEUCE: 75 YEARS OF THE '32 FORD

It was a bold move to think that a V-8 engine could be built inexpensively, especially in the midst of a depression. But Henry Ford wasn't the kind of man to accept the misgivings of those who said it couldn't, or shouldn't, be done. His amazing mechanical aptitude and the immense technical and financial resources of the Ford Motor Company would be the keys to solving any problem that might arise during the design of the new V-8 engine. But while Ford was a big-picture visionary, he tended to inflict his personal biases into the design of small components, often hindering progress.

Prior to 1932, there were only a few cars that used V-8 power. Most automotive engines at that time were inline fours, with inline sixes and inline eights making up much of the rest of the market. In 1917 Chevrolet introduced its 288 cubic inch, 55-horsepower V-8. The cost of a Series D 1917 Chevrolet with its new V-8 was $1,550. This new engine featured overhead valves on removable cylinder heads. But it lasted only two years. The 1921 Lincoln offered an 81-horsepower, 356-cubic inch V-8. The oversized 1923 Apperson also offered a V-8. All of these V-8 powered cars were three to twenty times the cost of a 20s-era Model T.

Ford engineers had been tinkering with V-8 engine designs as far back as 1922. It wasn't until 1929 that Henry Ford gave them marching orders to actually build one. Ford dictated that the valves be in the block. That meant that the engine would be a "flathead" design.

By 1925, America's appetite for V-8s had cooled and many companies were still installing straight eights. Duesenberg offered a 265-horsepower straight eight, Lincoln's V-8 grew to 385 cubic inches, and Cadillac's increased to 341 cubic inches. The inline engines were less expensive to produce than a V-8, but both configurations provided plenty of torque, which was necessary for the heavy luxury cars of the time. They needed the power of a big engine just to get them moving. Then there was the matter of driving comfort. All cars at that time were manual shift, which meant that in an underpowered car, the driver had to do a lot of shifting to maintain speed. The massive amount of torque produced by the straight eights and V-8s allowed drivers of these cars to slow down in traffic and resume speed without downshifting. This was seen as an important benefit to the wealthy, who found the act of shifting a tiresome chore better left to the chumps still driving Model Ts.

The V-8 engines in these large cars were expensive to build because of their many parts. Plus, they were very heavy. The extra cost and weight of these early V-8s were not detrimental to a heavy, expensive luxury car, but in a car built for the masses, something less expensive and simpler was required.

Henry Ford wanted to remain competitive in the automotive market and the trend was toward larger and heavier cars. He knew he needed to offer something better than the trusty four-cylinder, but he had never been fascinated with the inline six-cylinder engine. He felt, for example, that the crankshaft was too long to be reliable. As early as 1922 there had been experiments with various engine designs within Ford Motor Company, but it wasn't until 1929 that Henry Ford made the final decision to build a V-8. The program officially began when he ordered engineer Fred Thoms to go to the local junkyards and buy all of the V-8 engines he could find.

Fred Thoms returned with nine V-8 engines from such makes as Oldsmobile, Viking, and Cadillac—engines all constructed with multi-piece blocks. He also found two V-8s from Oldsmobile and Pontiac that were of a mono-block design. This was the design Ford was most interested in because the multi-piece designs carried higher manufacturing costs. He wanted a simple, low-cost design that would allow him to produce more V-8 engines in one day than his competitors could produce in a year. It also had to be built for a fraction of the cost of the competitor's engines.

By 1930, there were several small groups working on multiple V-8 engine designs within Ford. These groups worked independently of each other because Henry Ford wanted to keep the project a secret.

CHAPTER THREE

Ford's design criteria for the new V-8 stipulated that the valves had to be in the block. Overhead-valve designs added complexity and cost that Ford wanted to avoid. He also wanted the exhaust to exit from the side of the block. Other contemporary V-8 engines with in-block valves of the era needed a rat's nest of intake and exhaust tubing running through the engine's center valley, making for a complex and costly design.

Ford also dictated an offset crankshaft that provided no real-world benefit, as well as the use of existing water pump components to create the new V-8 pumps. Ford's insistence that these water pumps be mounted on the upper portion of the engine to draw out hot water proved to be folly. It is much harder to draw warm water than push cold water. Also, the top of the engine is where the water would be the hottest. Once it started to boil, all the pumps could do was draw steam while the engine continued to cook. Ford also rejected the installation of a thermostat. He felt that they were as unreliable as hydraulic brakes (another innovation that Ford resisted until 1939). These requirements, along with the fact that the exhaust was ported through the block, resulted in a number of overheating problems for the new engine.

One team worked on a 60-degree, 299 cubic inch V-8 with a bore and stroke of 3.625 inches. Ford directed the team to build the engine without an oil pump, using the flywheel to move oil up to a tank that would lubricate the bearings. This engine quickly failed.

The next problem that the engineers tackled was the fuel delivery system. The location of the fuel tank on the Model A had been in the cowl. No fuel pump was required, since gravity carried the fuel down to the carburetor. On the new 1932 Ford, however, the fuel tank would be moved to the rear of the car, opening up the

Initially, Henry Ford did not want to install a thermostat on the new V-8. He also insisted that the water pumps, one on each cylinder head, be mounted high on the engine. This is the pump on the left hand head.

The gas tank on the 1932 Ford was mounted in the rear of the car. Initially, Henry Ford did not want a fuel pump to draw gasoline to the engine. He asked his engineers to work on a carburetor that would pull the fuel that distance. He finally relented and Ford engineers mounted the fuel pump on the top-rear of the intake manifold. The petcock was used to drain out any sediment or water from the pump. Ford also used this fuel pump on the Model B engine. The V-8 fuel pump's location on the top of the engine meant that it was subjected to a great deal of heat, which often resulted in vapor lock as the fuel percolated inside the pump.

The carburetor that Ford installed on its first V-8s was a single-barrel downdraft design with a 1-1/4-inch diameter throat. Detroit Lubricator and Ford Motor Company manufactured these carburetors. Ford built the carburetor on this particular '32 Ford V-8.

cowl area for a fresh air vent. Henry Ford resisted the idea of a fuel pump and had his engineers work with carburetor designs that would provide adequate suction to pull the fuel the distance of the length of the car. This design quickly failed in real-world testing. Engineers bounced around the idea of pressurizing the fuel tank, but this idea soon fell off the table. A fuel pump on the new V-8 was eventually added and positioned on top of the rear portion of the intake manifold. In this location the pump was subjected to a great deal of heat; the term "vapor lock" soon became part of any V-8 owner's vocabulary.

Ford engineers used the same basic fuel pump on the V-8 and four-cylinder engine. The V-8 fuel pump was driven by a pushrod that rode on an eccentric lobe located on the rear of the camshaft. The four-cylinder engine's pump used a rocker arm that rode on the cam's eccentric lobe. The pump also contained a sediment chamber that had to be drained every 1,000 miles to remove any accumulated water or dirt from the pump.

One of Ford's V-8 engine design teams worked in Thomas Edison's old laboratory, which had been moved

By installing a V-8 instead of a straight six or eight, Ford did not have to lengthen the car's engine compartment. Ford's compact V-8 engine was not any longer than the four. The firewall on all 1932 Ford models was painted black.

from Florida to Ford's Greenfield Village Museum in Dearborn. Carl Schultz and Ray Laird comprised the team, with Emil Zoerlein joining to design the new V-8's ignition. Ford wanted a system that would last the life of the car. Henry also wanted the distributor driven directly off of the camshaft, instead of using a geared drive; he also wanted the distributor to be a single unit

CHAPTER THREE

that contained the coil. This distributor was designed with dual points to increase the dwell time. This would give the new V-8 engine a hotter spark. The first V-8 distributors were designed with a centrifugal advance mechanism and a vacuum brake.

By late in 1930, the team of Schultz and Laird had developed two 90-degree V-8 engines. One featured the same 299 cubic inch displacement as the earlier 60-degree design and another displaced 233 cubic inches with a 3.375-inch bore and 3.25-inch stroke. Henry Ford selected the 233 cubic inch design as the company's new V-8. In early 1931, the Rouge plant's foundry soon cast a few experimental engines that became known as "Model 24s." The first of these V-8s ran on a test stand in the back of the lab. Several others were installed in Model As for road testing. Road test procedures were as unsophisticated as the cars themselves and little was learned. Therefore, despite Ford's compulsory secrecy of the V-8 project, he decided to send a pair of the engines to Ford's dynamometer building for further testing. This testing confirmed that an oil pump was needed if Ford expected the new V-8 engines to survive. A pump driven off the camshaft was installed, solving the oiling problem. The dynamometer also gave engineers a chance to work on the roughness that plagued the engine. Many modifications were made to the carburetor and ignition curve to smooth the engine.

While the testing continued, the engine was also being redesigned. The original bore and stroke was changed, dropping the displacement to the eventual production 221 cubic inches. The new bore was downsized to 3.0625 inches and the stroke increased to 3.75 inches. The Model 24 engines had unique exhaust porting, with ports exiting the front and rear of the block. With smaller bores, there would be enough room to route all the exhaust passages inside the block, between the bores, to the side of the block. With a lot of tuning, this engine produced 65 horsepower. While not perfect, Henry Ford's new V-8 was ready for production.

Designing and building prototypes was easier than producing a production engine on a daily basis. But Henry Ford had the Rouge plant at his disposal—the largest industrial complex in the world. At this facility Ford workers turned iron ore into new car fenders, sand into glass, and would soon be producing the first low-price V-8 engines. Model T and Model A blocks were cast in the Rouge plant. But their construction

Automation had always been the key to America's industrial revolution. Ford used this device to gang-machine all of the valve seats on one side of its new V-8 engine. Once one side was complete, the block was rotated and the valve seats on the other side of the block would be machined.

was simple when compared to the casting required for the new V-8's block.

Sand molds are required to cast an iron cylinder block. These molds are constructed of "greensand." It retains its shape while the mold is being filled and then

60 ■ DEUCE: 75 YEARS OF THE '32 FORD

THE NEW V-8

This beautiful cutaway engine reveals the impressive inner workings of Ford's new V-8 engine and transmission. This same basic engine design would be in production for 21 years.

Henry Ford poses with his revolutionary V-8 engine. Ford's cash reserves and the industrial might of his massive Rouge plant allowed for the development of this engine.

61 ■ DEUCE: 75 YEARS OF THE '32 FORD

CHAPTER THREE

This is the left side of Ford's new V-8 as installed in a new 1932 Ford. This particularly well-preserved original engine has never been out of its chassis. Ford used green paint for the engine's cylinder heads, water pumps, and block. The intake manifold has a natural aluminum finish.

The right side of the 1932 Ford V-8 reveals the starter just below the log-style exhaust manifold. The generator is post-mounted at the front of the intake manifold. The line coming from the upper radiator hose is the connection for the optional water temperature gauge.

after the cast iron has cooled, the sand mold can be collapsed and the sand shaken out. Then the greensand is recycled to make another mold. Placement of the cores for the molds of a Model A block were not complicated and a slight shift of one of the cores didn't require the block to be scrapped. The new V-8 required more than 50 greensand mold cores to be accurately positioned. This was especially critical for the exhaust passages that snaked in between the bores. Initially, the rate of scrap blocks was exceptionally high—in some cases 100% of a day's production run. In addition to the shifting cores, the composition of the cast iron alloy was often not correct, thus creating more scrap. Foundry workers suddenly had much more precise parts to make, and had a much smaller margin for error. Ford quickly found that this new V-8 block could not be cast the same way as a four-cylinder engine.

To properly cast the new V-8 block, Ford engineers had to create fixtures to ensure that the cores were placed correctly. The methods for making the greensand cores were changed from a process done by hand to an automated method. This ensured that the cores were properly compacted. Ford engineers also created standards for checking the composition of the cast

Henry Ford (far right) stands with a few of his engineers looking over the installation of one of the new V-8s in a '32 chassis. The new V-8 engine displaced 221 cubic inches. With minor modifications, this engine would be produced through 1939.

62 ■ DEUCE: 75 YEARS OF THE '32 FORD

THE NEW V-8

There were only two outward indicators that a 1932 Ford was powered by a new V-8: the V-8 hubcaps and the small V-8 emblem on the center of the headlight bar. Another clue was the V-8's purring exhaust tone.

iron alloy to reduce defects due to materials. By the end of March 1932, the Rouge foundry was producing 100 blocks a day. By July, production of the V-8s reached 3,000.

Ford's new V-8 engine required several types of new machines to make the engine's bores, valve seats, and bearing mounts. The rigidity of the new block allowed both banks of cylinders to be machined simultaneously. Once machined, the early production blocks went to the old Edison lab for assembly. As production increased, the engine assembly moved into the Rouge plant. In

It's March 9, 1932, and Henry Ford is personally stamping the first production V-8 engine with the VIN 18-1. On this particular day 19 V-8 cars were built. The engine that Henry stamped was later pulled and is currently on display in the Henry Ford Museum in Dearborn, Michigan.

63 ■ DEUCE: 75 YEARS OF THE '32 FORD

CHAPTER THREE

Hot rodders quickly fell in love with Ford's new V-8 engine. The aftermarket industry quickly embraced the flathead and offered a wide variety of hop-up components. This particular 1950 Merc flathead was built by Mark Kirby for Jon Hall's five-window coupe. It's topped with Edelbrock heads and intake manifold.

One of the first performance-enhancing intake manifolds produced was this Edelbrock "slingshot" manifold that mounted a pair of two-barrel carburetors.

addition to Ford's internal capacity to build parts, numerous automotive suppliers in the area built many of the engine's smaller components.

All new Ford V-8 cast iron components were painted Ford Engine Green, the same color as the Model A engine. The cast aluminum parts, the largest being the oil pan, were installed unpainted. Any stamped or forged parts were painted black. All of the new V-8s were stamped on the top of the flywheel cover in a sequence that started with "18-1." Henry Ford personally stamped the first production line-installed V-8 on March 9, 1932. That engine, test engine #243 as stamped on the top of the block, now resides in the Henry Ford Museum.

Throughout 1932, Ford made constant changes to the V-8 engine to fix problems and to improve durability and performance. The major changes to the block in 1932 included a revision to the bore dimension tolerance, a revised hole diameter for the fuel pump push rod bushing, and a change in the flange around the oil pump to improve sealing with the new stamped oil pan. Ford also incorporated a pair of "steady rods" into the flywheel housing. At the same time the dipstick was moved from the right side of the engine to the left.

Mounted on top of this 21-stud flathead engine is a rare Davies side-by-side intake manifold. These prewar manifolds were originally designed for Winfield carburetors, but this one has been modified for Stromberg 97s.

THE NEW V-8

Ford continued to build the 221 cubic inch flathead through the 1939 model year. The final version developed 85 horsepower. As new models became larger and heavier, it became necessary for Ford to redesign the flathead for additional displacement. The new flathead, first seen in the 1938 Ford, displaced 239.4 cubic inches and developed 95 horsepower. In addition to having greater displacement than the 221 cubic-inch engine, the new flathead could be distinguished by the 24 studs used to hold each head in place. In 1949, Ford released its last version of the flathead that displaced 255.4 cubic inches. This engine would be used in Mercury passenger cars through the end of production in 1953. During that time period, Ford cars used the 239.4 cubic inch version. The flathead engines produced between 1949 and 1953 can be easily spotted— they lack an integral bellhousing that all earlier engines had.

Ford also created a downsized version of the flathead that displaced 136 cubic inches. It was used between 1937 and 1940. Ford rated the engine at 60 horsepower and it soon became to be known as the "V8 60." As a passenger car engine, it proved to be too small. It performed well in midget racecars, however, so aftermarket suppliers built a lot of speed equipment for this engine.

The highest degree of flathead engine development came from an unlikely duo born in Belgium, educated in Germany, and raised in Russia—the Duntov brothers, Zora and Yura. They initially developed the famed Ardun heads to solve a problem with Ford's flathead truck engines. These aluminum heads featured a hemispherical combustion chamber and overhead valves. Physically too big for a passenger car engine compartment, these aftermarket heads never found a market until they were discovered by C-T Automotive's Don Clark and Clem Tebow. They found that the Ardun-equipped flathead fit nicely in Clark's '32 Ford Roadster. With a little development work they were able to run this roadster over 160 miles per hour at Bonneville. Today, a hot rod with Ardun heads on a flathead engine is highly regarded.

The Ford flathead V-8 engine proved to be the hot rodding standard until it was overshadowed by the small-block Chevrolet V-8 in 1955. Today, the flathead is seeing a resurgence in the hot-rodding world. Once overshadowed by slick overhead V-8s, many owners are realizing that the flathead may not be as powerful, but it has decades of hot rodding history on its résumé. It also sounds and looks completely different than any other V-8.

The ultimate in flathead engine development was the Ardun head design of two European brothers, Zora and Yura Duntov. They created an overhead hemi conversion that made an amazing amount of power. Initially designed to improve truck engines, the conversions were quickly embraced by hot rodders.

CHAPTER THREE

V-8 Engine Specifications

Horsepower	65 @ 3,400 rpm
Bore	3.062 inches
Stroke	3.750 inches
Displacement	221 cubic inches
Cylinders	8
Type	V-90 degree
Firing order	1-5-4-8-6-3-7-2
Valve arrangement	L
Valve type	Mushroom design (chromium and nickel alloy)
Tappet clearance	.013–.014-inch
Camshaft material	Carbon manganese steel forging
Crankcase capacity	5 quarts
Oil pump drive	Gear from camshaft
Water pumps	Centrifugal (one in each head)
Compression ratio	5.5 to 1
Pistons	Heat-treated aluminum alloy
Number of rings	3
Crankshaft material	Carbon manganese steel
Crankshaft weight	65 pounds
Crankshaft main bearings	3
Crankshaft bearing material	Babbitt
Connecting rod length	7 inches
Connecting rod material	Steel forgings ("I" beam section)
Carburetor type	Down-draft single throat
Carburetor manufacturer	Detroit Lubricator
Clutch type	Single driven dry disc
Clutch diameter	9-inch
Clutch facing material	Asbestos composition
Engine suspension	3 points
Weight with transmission and clutch	615 pounds

The Model B Four

Ford had built its automotive reputation on its reliable four-cylinder engine. Some customers felt that the extra cost of a V-8 didn't justify any improvement in performance, if it meant a possible loss of reliability. For those individuals, Ford improved its Model A engine for 1932 and called it the "B" engine. With the slightly larger '32s and the more powerful base engines being offered by the competition, it was only natural that Ford would upgrade its durable four. This engine would continue to be offered, in dwindling numbers, in Ford passenger cars through the 1934 model year—closing out 26 years of dependable service.

The last version of Ford's Model A four-cylinder engine displaced 200.5 cubic inches and developed 40 horsepower at 2,000 rpm. This engine had a bore of 3.88 inches and a stroke of 4.25 inches. This engine proved to be completely adequate to push a 2,800-pound Model A down the road.

THE NEW V-8

While the bore and stroke remained the same, Ford engineers added a new head design, a revised camshaft, improved fuel delivery and a revised ignition curve to increase the horsepower by 25 to 50 percent over the Model A version. The changes to the block consisted of an added boss on the right side for the mounting of the mechanical fuel pump, larger main bearings, and an improved oiling system that eliminated the external oil return line. The head featured a revised combustion chamber that raised the compression ratio to 4.6:1, up from 4.2:1 used in the Model A. The only visual changes made to the head was the addition of the letter "C" cast onto the top surface and a revision to the water outlet. The crankshaft was forged, similar to the Model A, but had larger diameter journals. Ford engineers also revised the camshaft profile on both the intake and exhaust. The Zenith updraft carburetor was larger and had a revised float bowl. Similar to the 1932 V-8s, the Model B four-cylinder engines were painted Ford Engine Green.

Ford changed the location of the engine numbers on the four-cylinder from the side of the engine, as had been done on the Model As, to the top of the flywheel housing, as was being done on the new V-8s. While the V-8 numbers started with number 1, the B engines were continued from the Model A's numbering sequence with the first B engine stamped 5,000,000. Early production engine

Ford improved its reliable four-cylinder engine for its 1932 line of cars. Ford engineers took the basic Model A engine and increased the displacement to 200.5 cubic inches and added a new cylinder head. This revised engine, now called a Model B, developed 50 horsepower at 2,800 rpm.

Four-Cylinder Engine Specifications

Horsepower	50 @ 2,800 rpm
Bore	3.375 inches
Stroke	4.250 inches
Displacement	200.5 cubic inches
Cylinders	4
Type	Inline four
Firing order	1-2-4-3
Valve arrangement	L
Valve type	Mushroom (chromium and nickel alloy)
Camshaft material	Carbon manganese steel
Crankcase capacity	5 quarts
Oil pump drive	Gear
Water pump	Centrifugal (front of cylinder head)
Compression ratio	4.6 to 1
Pistons	Heat treated aluminum alloy
Number of rings	3
Crankshaft material	Carbon manganese steel
Crankshaft weight	38 pounds
Crankshaft main bearings	3
Connecting rod length	7.5 inches
Connecting rod material	Steel forgings ("I" beam section)
Carburetor type	Up-draft single throat
Carburetor manufacturer	Zenith
Clutch type	Single driven dry disc
Clutch diameter	9 inches
Clutch facing material	Asbestos composition
Engine suspension	3 points
Weight with transmission and clutch	464 pounds

numbers for the passenger cars had the prefix of "AB" and that was changed in mid-April to a single "B" prefix.

Ford engineers designed a unique piece of hardware for the four-cylinder installation in the 1932 Ford. In addition to the engine's mounts, engineers installed a vibration snubber between the firewall and the back of the engine. This snubber assembly consisted of a large stamping that attached to the firewall. Within this assembly were felt-cushioned friction surfaces that attached to the rear of the block. The spring tension on the friction surfaces could be adjusted to dampen the engine's side-to-side movement.

The Model B engine was produced through the 1934 model year. The buying public had grown to love Ford's new V-8 and there was no longer a need for a four-cylinder engine. This basic four-cylinder engine powered millions of Ford cars and trucks. Ford had created a simple design that proved to be exceptionally sturdy.

Henry Ford was wise enough to know that he had to do something special to stay in the automotive market in 1932. A new body style would not be enough to compete against the hot selling Chevrolet and its six-cylinder engine. His own personal prejudice against the longer crankshaft required in an inline six or eight was

THE NEW V-8

Ford painted the Model B four-cylinder engine the same shade of Ford Engine Green as the V-8. This engine would continue to be installed in Ford passenger cars, albeit in constantly reducing numbers, through the 1934 model year.

a precipitating factor in his decision to go with the compact V-8 design. Henry Ford also had the industrial might of the massive Rouge plant at his disposal. In the midst of a depression, he made the bold move to create a V-8 engine for the masses. While not perfect upon its release, the new V-8 soon became the performance standard in the low-price field and served Ford well for 21 years. He also kept his previous customers happy by offering an improved version of his four-cylinder engine in the new models. In any normal economy, Ford should have done exceptionally well, but in the midst of a depression it was going to be tough to sell any car, be it V-8 or four cylinder.

The Model B four-cylinder engine used a Zenith updraft single barrel carburetor. A mechanical fuel pump mounted on the block fed the carburetor. Barely visible behind the cylinder head is the engine vibration dampener that Ford engineers mounted on the firewall.

69 ■ DEUCE: 75 YEARS OF THE '32 FORD

CHAPTER FOUR

Ford's 1932 Open Cars: Roadsters, Phaetons & Cabriolets

Roadsters were at the forefront of early automotive design. They were less complex than a closed car and therefore less costly. Roadsters offered the open-air feel and wind-in-your-face freedom of the road to the driving public. This Deluxe Ford Roadster demonstrates how attractive motoring could be in 1932.

FORD'S 1932 OPEN CARS: ROADSTERS, PHAETONS & CABRIOLETS

The very first automobiles were open cars—not much more than a simple open wagon powered by an internal combustion engine, instead of a horse. From this open wagon design came the Roadster and the Phaeton. Early Roadsters featured a small windscreen, seating for two, and no side windows. Because it took less time and money to manufacture a Roadster, these vehicles sold for less. Because the Phaeton seated more people, it was slightly more expensive than the Roadster. However, the real price paid by the buyer was the constant exposure to the elements. In the western and southern states with more temperate climates, open cars sold well. As the closed coupe and sedan developed, more northern buyers opted for them and for the protection they offered. But there has always been a market for an open car, simply because people love to ride with the top down.

1932 Ford Roadster

Auto manufacturers in the early 1930s were designing and producing bigger automobiles. Ford's 1932 Roadster was no exception. The biggest difference between a 1932 Ford body and that of a Model A is its relative size. The 1928 Model A pioneered the installation of a rumble seat at Ford and they would be available

Ford offered its roadster in both Standard and Deluxe versions. The Deluxe Roadster was recognized by its tan top and cowl lights; Standard models had a black top and no cowl lights.

71 ■ DEUCE: 75 YEARS OF THE '32 FORD

CHAPTER FOUR

Ford included the rumble seat as a standard feature of every 1932 Roadster. A luggage compartment was optional. The rear deck lid (with either rumble seat or luggage compartment) was interchangeable between the five-window coupe, Sport Coupe, and Cabriolet models.

on Model As through the end of production in 1931. Engineers also added an optional rumble seat for 1932. Another visual difference between the Model A and the 1932 Ford Roadster body was the slight kick-up in the rear of the '32 for the gas tank. The lower edge of the Model A body from the cowl to the rear followed a straight line. The 1932 Ford's body character lines were also more pronounced.

The front floor on all 1932 Ford Roadsters was covered with a tan rubber mat. The door trim panels on both the Deluxe and Standard models included a storage pocket with a flap that snapped shut.

72 ■ DEUCE: 75 YEARS OF THE '32 FORD

FORD'S 1932 OPEN CARS: ROADSTERS, PHAETONS & CABRIOLETS

All 1932 Ford Roadsters were fitted with these small chrome-plated devices. Most people think they are grab handles for rumble seat passengers, but they are actually rests for when the top is folded back.

The rear panel on the 1932 Ford Roadster's top could be opened so rumble seat passengers could talk to those in the main passenger compartment. The top could be folded back or removed completely.

One of the most beautiful aspects of the 1932 Ford Roadster body is its rear wheel opening. Ford designers added what appears to be a flare to the body molding around the rear fender. This area is flatter on all the other bodies.

73 ■ DEUCE: 75 YEARS OF THE '32 FORD

These two young ladies are out for a ride in their new 1932 Deluxe Ford Roadster. They're about to have their stylish hats blown off because they have folded the windshield flat, a feature of all 1932 Roadsters and Phaetons.

Ford offered two Roadster models in 1932: the Standard Roadster and the Deluxe Roadster. Ford's Deluxe Roadster model included a rumble seat, cowl lights, and an upgraded interior with Copra Drab fine colonial leather and wood-grained finished instrument panels. Wind wings that were initially installed on both Standard and Deluxe Roadster models became a Deluxe-only feature later in production. The visible top irons were chrome-plated on the Deluxe model with the others painted Golden Beryl, but on the Standard versions they were simply painted black. Ford also used a tan material for the tops on its Deluxe models but a black material was used on the Standard Roadsters. The Standard Model B Roadster listed for $449.25 and a V-8 model was priced at $499.25. The B-model Deluxe Roadster sold for $489.25 and the V-8 version cost $539.25. All of these Ford Roadster models were less expensive than equivalent models offered by Chevrolet or Plymouth. Ford's strategy was to undercut the

This 1932 Ford Standard Roadster fire chief's car, from the city of Piedmont, California, has been outfitted with a siren, red lights, and several aftermarket accessories. Its body is painted a non-standard color (sans pin stripes) and was most likely done by the local dealer to the department's specs.

FORD'S 1932 OPEN CARS: ROADSTERS, PHAETONS & CABRIOLETS

The 1932 Ford Cabriolet offered the buyer the open-air feel of the roadster with the ability to close out the world with roll-up windows. A rumble seat was standard along with all of the features associated with any Deluxe model.

competition, sell more vehicles, and create a huge volume of production.

One styling feature of the new Ford Roadster that did not appear on any other 1932 Ford body was the elegantly shaped quarter panel. The area from the belt line to the top of the wheel opening appears to be slightly concave. The body molding over the wheel opening appears more pronounced than on the other 1932 Ford bodies, giving the rear wheel opening on the body a virtual flared look. This unusual feature sets the Roadster apart from all other body styles, especially in the hot-rodding world.

1932 Ford Cabriolet

Ford's 1932 Cabriolet was an unusual model because it was a true convertible. It featured a foldable soft top and roll-up windows. Ford offered its Cabriolet in one model that contained all the Deluxe features, including cowl lights, ashtrays, and either Bedford Cord cloth or genuine leather upholstery for the interior. It also featured a chrome windshield frame, full safety glass, and a standard rumble seat. The Cabriolet's windshield was surrounded by body structure that extended up from the cowl. Its chrome windshield frame featured squared upper corners and was not hinged at the top. The

This early production 1932 Ford Cabriolet was shot at Ford's Rouge plant complex. Its windshield frame and door window frames were chrome plated. The exterior door handle is in the same below-the-belt-line location as the roadster, but the style of the handle is the same as those used on closed cars.

75 ■ DEUCE: 75 YEARS OF THE '32 FORD

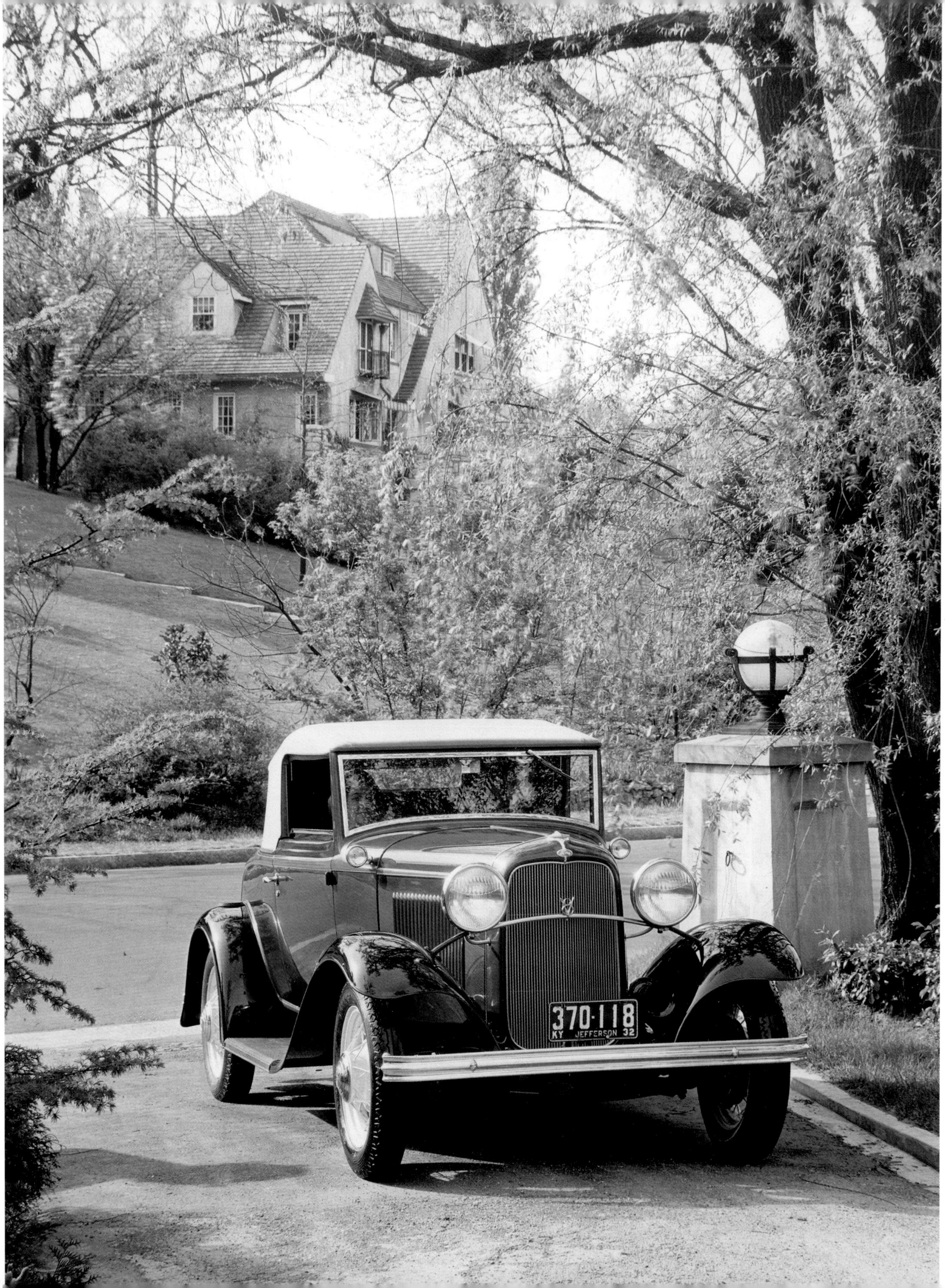
370·118
KY JEFFERSON 32

FORD'S 1932 OPEN CARS: ROADSTERS, PHAETONS & CABRIOLETS

Left: The 1932 Ford Cabriolet's cowl top and windshield structure were the same as used on the B-400 convertible sedan. The Cabriolet's doors and door glass were unique and not used on any other model.

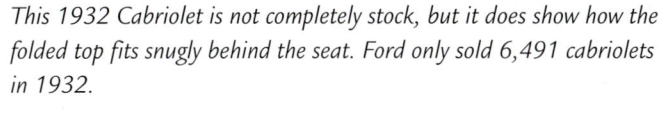

This 1932 Cabriolet is not completely stock, but it does show how the folded top fits snugly behind the seat. Ford only sold 6,491 cabriolets in 1932.

Ford wood-grained the Cabriolet's instrument panel including the inside of the A-pillars and windshield header. The single vacuum-operated windshield wiper motor is mounted to the inside of the header.

well-trimmed soft top could be folded back and into a well. Ford included a special boot to cover the folded top.

Ford added unique doors to the Cabriolet. The exterior door handles were the same as those used on closed cars, but they were not mounted along the beltline as those on the closed cars. They were mounted below the beltline in the same location as the exterior door handles on the Roadster. This lack of interchangeability between models is hard to understand, given Henry Ford's usual preference for standardized components that facilitated the assembly line process.

77 ■ DEUCE: 75 YEARS OF THE '32 FORD

CHAPTER FOUR

In 1932, Ford sold 6,491 Cabriolets. While collectors love the elegant Cabriolet, hot rodders have traditionally shunned them. Early hot rodders would usually remove the windshields of their cars in order to race at the dry lakes, but the Cabriolet did not have an easily removable windshield. Its fixed windshield posts also created a problem for hot rodders who wanted to chop the top. One notable example is the 2005 Dearborn Deuce '32 Ford body, which has taken the best of the original Cabriolet to create a Roadster with a folding top. This body is extensively covered in Chapter 7.

1932 Ford Phaeton

The Phaeton was the "family-sized," four-door version of the Roadster. While still an open car, it could seat five comfortably. Ford added a folding top and side curtains to protect the driver and passengers from the elements. And like

Ford offered both Standard and Deluxe Phaeton models in 1932. Each comfortably seated five. This is a Deluxe model with cowl lights and, like the Deluxe Roadsters, the top was also covered with a tan material. The Phaeton used the same chrome windshield frame as the Roadster.

78 ■ DEUCE: 75 YEARS OF THE '32 FORD

FORD'S 1932 OPEN CARS: ROADSTERS, PHAETONS & CABRIOLETS

This factory-fresh Deluxe V-8 Phaeton listed for $584.25 and was one of the lowest-priced models Ford offered in 1932. The front doors on the Phaetons were identical to the doors on a roadster.

the Roadster, Ford offered the Phaeton in a Standard and a Deluxe model. The Deluxe Phaeton featured the same cowl lights and interior upgrades as the Deluxe Roadster along with the tan top material and wind wings. The Standard B model listed for $484.25 and the Standard Phaeton with a V-8 listed for $534.25. The Phaeton in Deluxe trim with the B engine listed for $534.25 and the Deluxe with a V-8 sold for $584.25. The only 1932 Ford automobile less expensive than the Phaeton was the Roadster.

The Roadster and Phaeton bodies had much in common. The Roadster's doors and the Phaeton's front doors used identical inner panels and hardware, but the exterior skins were unique. They also shared the same windshield assemblies and cowl sheet metal. The windshield on both models could be folded forward onto the cowl. Initially, windshield wings were standard on all Roadster and Phaeton models. But in April 1932 they became optional on the Standard models.

The top has been folded back on this Deluxe Phaeton. Ford included what they called a "dust hood" for the top when it was in its folded position.

DEUCE: 75 YEARS OF THE '32 FORD

CHAPTER FOUR

This 1932 Ford Phaeton is equipped with the optional rear luggage rack. When this luggage rack was installed it required the relocation of the spare tire to the side. This Phaeton has twin side mounts and the dealer-installed right-hand taillight.

It must have been hard for someone looking at a new Deluxe Phaeton in a dealership to resist such a luxurious leather interior. While the wool tapestry carpeting looks wonderful, all Phaetons, even the Deluxe models, were fitted with front and rear tan rubber floor mats.

Ford trimmed the interior of its Phaeton and Roadster in similar weather-resistant materials. The seats in the Standard model were covered with two-tone, black-brown, Colonial Grain Artificial Leather with the instrument panel painted Interior Gray. The floors were covered with a rubber mat. The seats in the Deluxe version were covered in real leather. Ford offered the rumble seat as an option on the Roadster and trimmed it with two-tone black-brown Colonial Grain Artificial Leather

80 ■ DEUCE: 75 YEARS OF THE '32 FORD

FORD'S 1932 OPEN CARS: ROADSTERS, PHAETONS & CABRIOLETS

Ford pinstriped all 1932 Roadsters, Cabriolets, and Phaetons. The striping pattern on the Standard and Deluxe models was the same. There was a pair of 1/16-inch-wide stripes that followed the beltline and joined at the forward edge of the hood. A single stripe followed the lower body molding along the rocker panel and arched over the wheel openings. The exterior color of the body determined the color of the striping.

Hot Rod '32 Ford Roadsters

Hot rodders have always loved the 1932 Ford Roadster. Early roadsters that raced on California's dry lakes sowed the seeds of hot rodding. Roadsters were the preferred racecars for competing at the lakes, and Ford Roadsters made up the largest contingent of these racers. Competitors would strip off the fenders, headlights, and windshields and race across the dry lakebed at top speed. Ford produced other Roadster models that were popular with racers, but the 1932 model always held a special place in racers' hearts.

When they first came out, the new Fords must have been coveted for their more powerful B engine and interesting new V-8. But during the depression few rodders could afford a new 1932 Ford. Most waited for the wrecks to hit the junkyard. Initially, hot rodders who could afford a '32 most likely preferred the four-cylinder B engine because of the availability of speed equipment already on the shelf for that engine. Speed equipment was eventually developed for the V-8, and this sparked and nurtured the love affair that hot rodders had with the flathead, which continues to this day.

World War II put car production and hot rodding on hold. During this time, America's young men were serving their country either overseas or in many of America's defense plants. In both arenas they were learning skills that would advance the hot-rodding phenomenon. After the war many young men pulled their roadsters out of storage and picked up where they had left off years earlier.

After the war, auto manufacturers shifted from building tanks and bombers back to building automobiles. Pent up demand for new cars meant that the old cars that people had been driving throughout the war years were now relegated to used car lots or, in many cases, to the junkyard. Because Ford had used a durable, all-steel body, few cars lost their functionality even though paint had faded and engines needed rebuilding.

Deluxe Roadsters and Phaetons were fitted with chrome-plated top hardware. This Phaeton has a small fixture attached to the rear of the body where one of the top irons would rest when the top was folded.

Ford installed a wood-grained instrument panel on its Deluxe Phaetons. The lever on the steering wheel is the switch for the cowl lights and headlights. The button in the center is for the horn.

with a rubber floor mat. The folding top and dust hood were also made of similar materials between models. Early tops on the Standard models were covered with a black rubberized material. Later in the model year that was changed to black with a white interlined material. Deluxe tops were trimmed in the same tan material as the Deluxe Roadsters. The glass rear window and window frame were identical in all Roadster and Phaeton models. Side curtains were standard on both models.

CHAPTER FOUR

To run a roadster in an SCTA (Southern California Timing Association) event on the dry lakes, the windshield and headlights needed to be removed. Competitors also took off the fenders to eliminate the wind resistance they created. This 1932 Ford Roadster is typical of the cars that ran on the California lakes from the mid- to late-1940s. This competitor even re-grooved the rear tires for more traction.

The highly desirable 1932 Ford Roadsters were plentiful in Southern California and soon became hot rodding's vehicle of choice. A hot rodder could take advantage of the interchangeability of 1932 Ford components. For example, a hot rodder could buy a complete four-door sedan at a bargain price, discard the sedan body, and bolt on the Roadster body. This became a common phenomenon, as hot rodders turned forgotten 1932 Fords into hot rods built for speed.

In the mid and late 1940s, the roadster was the only body style accepted as a true hot rod. Coupes and sedans were pigeonholed as family cars that would never learn hot rodding's secret handshake. This preference for one body style over another was exceptionally clear in the Southern California Timing Association's (SCTA) early class structure, where there were no classes for coupes, but a class for every roadster. Helping to foster this bias was the huge number of roadsters on the West Coast. California's year-around good weather allowed the use of open cars almost every day of the year. California also had an unusual mix of people who added to the postwar interest in hot rodding. In addition to native Californians, there were the transplants from the depression-era dust bowl, adventurous types who had left their homes and God-forsaken land to go west in search of their fortune. Then there were military transplants who had spent a portion of their training on the West Coast and decided there were as many or more job opportunities in California as there were in Ohio or Wisconsin. The weather was better, too. The military also proved to be a great training ground for hot rodders. Young men returning from the war with advanced mechanical skills could apply their craft on fast hot rods instead of on fighter aircraft, maritime vessels, or other military vehicles.

California's dry lakes racers set the style for the 1932 Ford Roadster for decades to come. Cars with the fenders stripped off and the body up on the frame in its original position soon became known as "highboys." Once the car owner decided that the fenders would never go back on

The photo of this '32 highboy roadster was shot in 1952 at Paradise Mesa drag strip in San Diego, California. It features a filled grille shell, custom-louvered hood, an attractive headlight bar, and a mean looking set of lakes pipes. You can only imagine how jealous the other dogs must have been to see this one riding in a '32 Roadster.

CHAPTER FOUR

Bill Couch is a long-time hot rodder out of the Detroit area. He's owned this original roadster for decades. His two sons, John and Billy, recently pulled it out of the barn and made it driveable. This is John "dirt tracking" it around a corner.

Couch's roadster sits on an all-stock chassis right down to the mechanical brakes. Years ago much of the inner supporting structure of the body was cut away when it was used for drag racing.

FORD'S 1932 OPEN CARS: ROADSTERS, PHAETONS & CABRIOLETS

the car, they would fill the holes in the frame where the fenders had been attached. Hot rodders enhanced the 1932 grille shell by removing the Ford emblem and filling in the opening where the radiator cap poked through. Filling in the cowl vent was another common modification to the early 1932 Roadsters. Hot rodders most commonly removed the louvered panels from the side and added flat panels with no openings. This gave a highboy Roadster a cleaner look, but without the louvers the engine was prone to overheating. Racers often added new side panels with a different louver pattern offered by the factory. They also added louvers to the top of the hood.

Hot rodders made a number of changes to the 1932 Ford's hood. Early hot rod roadsters often ran without a

Ken Gross had Dave Simard construct what may be the finest traditionally styled modern-day '32 Ford Roadster. He's combined the best elements from the finest vintage '32 Roadsters with unparalleled workmanship to create his drop-dead gorgeous roadster.

85 ■ DEUCE: 75 YEARS OF THE '32 FORD

CHAPTER FOUR

A status symbol for any roadster owner is a headlight sticker from the L.A. Roadster show. This sticker allows the car into the inner sanctum of the show where all of the roadsters are parked. This '32 has attended four times.

The interior of Gross' '32 Roadster has the same classic look as the exterior. The seat and trim panel materials are leather and the carpet is wool. The instrument panel insert is from an Auburn.

hood, but a hood top was required for SCTA competition on the lakes. Competitors often left off the hood's sides and just ran with the top two sections. Others created a single-piece hood top from aluminum. This eliminated the hinge that ran down the center. Louvers were a big part of early hot rodding and the 1932 Roadster's hood provided an excellent canvas for the louver punch.

The lakes racers started another hot rodding trend that has lasted for decades—big and little tires. Hot rodders first put big tires on the rear wheels to effectively increase the rear end's gear ratio, resulting in a higher top speed. While this innovation was not first seen on the 1932 Ford, it worked exceptionally well with the overall car's design because of the large rear wheel openings. Another innovation from the

86 ■ DEUCE: 75 YEARS OF THE '32 FORD

FORD'S 1932 OPEN CARS: ROADSTERS, PHAETONS & CABRIOLETS

The engine in Gross' '32 Roadster is a supercharged flathead. While highly chromed and exceptionally clean, this car has seen lots of road miles.

The top piece on this vintage trophy from San Diego's Paradise Mesa drag strip confirms the appeal of the '32 highboy roadster in the mid-1950s.

world of hot rodding was the dropped front axle. The 1932 Ford's exceptionally strong front axle allowed hot rodders to heat and stretch the ends to move the spindles up in relation to the spring mount. This lowered the front end of the car, giving it a lower center of gravity and more stable handling. It also enhanced the car's forward rake that had been established by putting bigger tires on the rear wheels. The Ford Model T and A hot rods looked good with the staggered tire sizes and a nose-down attitude, but the 1932 Ford looked even better.

The 1932 Ford offered a stylish new frame on which those who owned a Model A could mount their Roadster body. The design of the frame and its larger cross section proved to be a more stable platform for these early Ford bodies than their original Model A frames. In addition, many hot rodders were enamored with the '32 Ford grille shell and added them to existing Model T and Model A hot rods. At speeds of 100 miles per hour or faster, the vertical bars in this stylish shell vibrated to create a unique and distinctive tone.

DEUCE: 75 YEARS OF THE '32 FORD

This '32 Ford Roadster is ready to race on the lakes. In case of a failure of its latches, the hood is also secured by a leather belt. It's interesting to see that this otherwise stock '32 highboy has a rolled rear pan.

It's a rarity to see a hot rodded 1932 Ford Cabriolet. This one was shot in 1952 at San Diego's Paradise Mesa drag strip. It's been chopped, but there is no windshield header, just the exposed edge of glass. It's been channeled and has a custom hood with lunch box latches holding on the top. The interior trim material has been rolled over the sides of the doors, over the back of the seat, and over the top well.

FORD'S 1932 OPEN CARS: ROADSTERS, PHAETONS & CABRIOLETS

The McGee and Spencer Roadsters

Two 1932 Ford Roadsters from the 1940s that established trends for legions of hot rod roadsters are the Bob McGee and Doane Spencer 1932 Roadsters. These cars took the best of what was being done by the lakes racers in the mid to late 1940s and translated it with outstanding workmanship into two of the finest hot rods ever built. On the surface, both are highboys, but the cars are decidedly different. McGee's car is smooth and stylish, while Spencer's roadster has a racy look.

Neither builder set out to make an iconic hot rod; they just took the best of what others had done before them and improved upon the theme. But it's almost impossible to build a highboy Roadster today without seeing the fingerprints of McGee or Spencer.

McGee started with his roadster in 1940. In 1941, he ran it at the lakes as a member of the Gear Grinders. McGee, like so many young men of that era, took up the call to arms and spent several years in the Pacific theater. While away, he loaned his car to a fellow club member who promptly wrecked it. His friend managed to get another roadster body and enough parts for McGee to rebuild his roadster after the war.

McGee's vision was of a car that was much lower than the roadsters of the era. In the front he used one of Ed Stewart's dropped front axles and reversed spring eyes. In the rear he Z-ed the frame and added a Model A crossmember. With 5.00 x 16 tires in the front and 7.00 x 16s in the rear, the car sat low with the mildest of rakes. The perfect stance and attention to design detail is demonstrated by the concentricity of the wheel opening lip on the quarter panel and the rear tire.

One other change McGee made to the '32 Roadster—and he may have been the first to do it—was to hide the door hinges. A few hot rodders molded the hinges into

Bob McGee's famous red '32 Roadster cast the mold for thousands of other '32 Ford Roadsters to be built in the future. Its lines were cleaned up by the use of hidden door hinges, hidden hood latches, and removal of the exterior door handles. McGee also built in a perfect stance.

CHAPTER FOUR

McGee topped his flathead engine with a pair of Federal Mogul copper heads. The black bar extending from the firewall to the grille shell contains the hood retention and latching system.

The lakes pipes on Bob McGee's roadster outline the character line in the frame. The fact that these pipes are black instead of chrome is one of the understated elements that make this roadster so appealing.

the doors, but no one had hidden them entirely. On today's vehicles, hidden door hinges are commonplace. This innovation was new to production cars at the time McGee built his roadster. To further emphasize clean lines, McGee removed the outer door handles—a common modification to hot rods then and now.

McGee made another major exterior modification to his roadster that has yet to be copied. He removed the panel below the deck lid and had a new deck lid made that ran down to the lower body reveal. It's a subtle modification that almost goes unnoticed because the license

FORD'S 1932 OPEN CARS: ROADSTERS, PHAETONS & CABRIOLETS

body color and had the interior and top stitched in tan to match the color of the leather interior.

Built as a driver, McGee used his roadster for transportation between 1947 and 1952. He drove it sporadically for the next two years and then sold it in 1955. The new owner got rid of the flathead and installed a small-block Chevy and then turned it over to Dick Scritchfield, who drove it, rented it to the movie studios, and raced it. After bouncing around between a few other owners, Bruce Meyer finally bought it in the late 1990s and restored it as McGee had first built the car.

Bruce Meyer also owns the other iconic 1932 Roadster built in the late 1940s—the Doane Spencer roadster. Spencer followed a different path when he built his roadster. Like McGee's car, Spencer's roadster was also rebuilt after the war. He initially bought the roadster in 1944 from an old friend as a full-fendered hot rod. The fenders were quickly stripped away and the metamorphosis began. The roadster already had a Duval windshield that came from Spencer a few years earlier. What's different about the installation on Spencer's roadster is the way the ends were reshaped and flared and the way the rear edge of the cowl was reformed. Both modifications are pleasing to the eye, but so subtle that even the trained "hot rod" eye may miss them.

McGee extended the deck lid down to include the body's lower rear panel. Mounted on the bottom edge of the deck lid are the license plate and unpretentious Pontiac taillights.

plate and round Pontiac taillights are mounted in the traditional locations.

McGee made other subtle modifications. He shortened the front frame horns and molded in a spreader bar with a V shape. He had a new hood made with a one-piece top and new sides. Both top and sides were louvered and the latches for the sides were hidden. He also filled the cowl vent. McGee chose a red lacquer for the

McGee had the interior of his roadster trimmed in tan leather. The steering column and wheel are out of a 1940 Ford. He veered from the norm and installed a custom-made instrument panel.

91 ■ DEUCE: 75 YEARS OF THE '32 FORD

CHAPTER FOUR

Inset: *Spencer installed Schroeder sprint car steering gear in his roadster. This required a hole on the side of the left cowl where the gear attached to the drag link. He finished it off with a stylish teardrop-shaped fairing.*

Doane Spencer built his black '32 Roadster with more of a racy look. He added a Duval windshield and cut off the front frame horns and installed a nerf bar.

Spencer's car took on a racy edge in 1950 when he decided to race it in the Mexican La Carrera Panamericana Road Race. He cut off the front and rear frame horns and Z-ed the frame. He also moved the gas tank into the trunk and added a Halibrand quick-change rear end. He intended to replace the flathead with a new Lincoln overhead V-8 for the race, but the engine's extra weight quickly became a bigger liability than the horsepower it could provide. Spencer decided upon one of Ford's new Y-block engines instead, but never actually installed one.

One of the most highly distinguishable changes Spencer made to his roadster was the addition of the Schroeder sprint car steering gear. This necessitated drilling a hole in the side of the left cowl for the drag link. Spencer didn't just have the end poking through an unfinished aperture; he created a small teardrop-shaped fairing for the side of the cowl. This same teardrop shape is seen where the hairpins mount to the frame. Spencer's other highly identifiable modification is the addition of lakes pipes, smoothly faired into the side of the frame. Another small but highly detailed addition for the race was a set of cooling scoops for the brakes. These and

FORD'S 1932 OPEN CARS: ROADSTERS, PHAETONS & CABRIOLETS

Spencer cut off the rear frame horns and Z-ed the rear of the frame to allow his roadster to sit lower. He added a small rolled pan to the rear of the body. Without the rear-mounted gas tank, the Halibrand quick-change rear end is easily seen.

The instrument panel of Doane Spencer's roadster, with its large collection of gauges, looked as if it could have been pulled out of a World War II bomber. The sprint car-style steering wheel completes the race-car look.

other small modifications made it unique and highly identifiable with its owner. But by the time the modifications were complete, the Mexican government canceled the race. In 1958, Spencer sold his roadster to Lynn Wineland, who later sold it to Neal East. East eventually sold it to Bruce Meyer, who restored it to its early 1950s look.

Pete Chapouris, hot rod builder and restorer of both the McGee and Spencer roadsters, says, "If I had a Deuce roadster it would be Doane Spencer's car. It's the car that had the most impact on me— it's one of the best cars ever built. The next one is Bob McGee's. The great irony is

93 ■ DEUCE: 75 YEARS OF THE '32 FORD

that 40 years later, I restored them for Bruce. It was a phenomenal turn-around."

The McGee and Spencer roadsters epitomize the iconic look of the 1932 Ford highboy roadster hot rod. Both have traditional hot rod modifications, but they also have several unique modifications. Both are extraordinary cars with exquisite details that have been restored and preserved as the soul of the 1932 Ford Roadster hot rod. "If you're going to build a Deuce roadster," says Chapouris, "it either looks like McGee's car (with horns and a gas tank in the back) or it looks like Spencer's car (with roll pans and no horns or gas tank). Those two cars set the tone for what a Deuce roadster should look like."

The 404 Roadster

In 1950, brothers Pat and Tony Berardini owned a muffler shop in South Central Los Angeles. Drag racing was starting to boom in Southern California at that time and they got the bug. Their muffler shop was the perfect location to build a racecar to promote their business.

The brothers selected a 1932 Roadster as the basis for a racecar that they intended to run in the Street Roadster class at the drags. With Pat doing the engineering and building, brother Tony did the driving. Pat added safety hubs to the rear axle long before they were required, as well as a roll bar of adequate height to protect his

When organized drag racing boomed onto the scene in the mid-1950s, it drew brothers Pat and Tony Berardini into the fold. They owned a muffler shop in Los Angeles and successfully raced this '32 Roadster in the Street Roadster class.

FORD'S 1932 OPEN CARS: ROADSTERS, PHAETONS & CABRIOLETS

The Berardini brothers ran a flathead engine in their roadster that pushed it to 111 miles per hour in the quarter mile. Today, this roadster is owned by Roger Morrison and was restored by Dave Crouse.

Fenders were a requirement of the Street Roadster class. The Berardini brothers added motorcycle fenders to the front and bobbed the stock rear fenders. The number 404 on the side was derived from the engine's then-new Isky 404 cam.

95 ■ DEUCE: 75 YEARS OF THE '32 FORD

CHAPTER FOUR

Safety regulations for drag racing in the 1950s required little more than a pair of seat belts. The seats are surplus aircraft units. The dash features an engine-tuned instrument panel and distinctive red and white Von Dutch pinstriping.

brother in case of a rollover accident. Because the Street Roadster class required fenders, they bobbed the stock rear fenders and added motorcycle fenders to the front. Pat finished the car in black with white flames highlighted by Von Dutch pinstriping. The car originally ran with the number 3 on the side, but the number 404 was added to the side in deference to the performance boost they got from the Iskenderian 404A cam they had installed in the roadster's flathead engine. The brothers raced at all of Southern California's drag strips. Driver Tony held up his end of the bargain by winning 80 percent of his races. In 1955, the Berardini brothers' 404 Roadster owned drag racing in Southern California, setting records at every strip and running speeds as high as 111 miles per hour. The brothers soon added a 1929 Roadster that ran successfully in the Altered class. Next door to the muffler shop was their used car business. They often parked the roadsters on the lot to attract potential customers.

In 1955, the 404 Roadster appeared briefly in the movie *Blackboard Jungle*. Later that year, the Berardini brothers advertised it for sale in *Drag News* for $975. It quickly sold to Jean LaCoste, of San Rafael, California (LaCoste is better known as "Jeano," a name given to him by an Italian friend). After removing the Bernardini

96 ■ DEUCE: 75 YEARS OF THE '32 FORD

FORD'S 1932 OPEN CARS: ROADSTERS, PHAETONS & CABRIOLETS

brothers' names from the car, he successfully drag raced it in Northern California, retaining the number 404 on the side and expanding the car's reputation. In 1960, LaCoste added a 1955 Chrysler 354-cubic-inch Hemi and painted over the Berardini brother's black and white colors with several coats of Goldenrod Yellow. Bowing to the roadster's racing heritage, LaCoste kept the big numbers 404 on the side. With the new engine, LaCoste set a speed record of 136.36 miles per hour at Half Moon Bay Drag Strip.

LaCoste sold the 404 Roadster to Rudy Perez in 1968 for $1,000. Perez removed the Chrysler engine and replaced it with a small-block Chevy, thereby converting the historic racecar into a street rod. He paid homage to the car's racing history by having the number 404 on his license plate. Perez drove the car for 37 years, racking up 185,702 miles. While he had vowed never to sell the car, Perez finally sold it to Roger Morrison, a collector from Salina, Kansas. Perez recognized that Morrison's intentions for the car were honorable.

Morrison turned the car over to Dave Crouse at his Custom Auto shop in Loveland, Colorado, for the restoration. His team of experts brought the Berardini brothers' 404 Roadster back to life. On January 19, 2004, it was unveiled at the NHRA museum with Pat Berardini, Jean LaCoste, and Rudy Perez in attendance. Shortly thereafter, it won the Bruce Meyer Preservation Award at the 2005 Grand National Roadster Show.

The story of the 1932 Ford Roadster continues today. It still remains the most popular starting point for a hot rod. The flathead-powered dry lakes pioneers cast the mold for modern hot rodders who today are running a

One of the joys of owning a hot rod is being able to personalize it with unique components. Paul Gommi added a vintage Pines Winter Front to his '32 Roadster. This rare aftermarket grille insert features thermostatically controlled grille bars that block off air going to the radiator when the engine is cold and open when the engine warms up.

97 ■ DEUCE: 75 YEARS OF THE '32 FORD

CHAPTER FOUR

Bob Everets stretched the wheelbase on his '32 Roadster by two inches. The engine is a vintage Dodge Red Ram Hemi. The original cowl vent must be removed when adding a Duval windshield. To keep a high level of airflow to the interior, he added two small cowl vents in front of the windshield. The attractive top is custom made.

Randy Fish's '32 Roadster has the smoothed-body look of Bob McGee's car with the addition of the sleek Duval windshield. He's also removed the front frame horns. Riding on top of the filled grille shell is a small "Fish fin," an homage to the owner's last name.

small-block Chevy, a vintage Hemi engine, or even Lexus power. The modifications they pioneered, such as smooth hood sides, big and little tire combinations, and the timeless highboy look, have been done again and again by modern builders. In true hot rod tradition, each builder adds something to personalize his or her creation. Every facet of the 1932 Ford Roadster has been altered slightly to create a unique look for each car. But each builder adheres to certain time-honored traditions: forward rake, chopped windshield, low seating position, and big and little tires.

Hot rods look good sitting still, but they look even better on the road moving at speed. Because nothing is hidden, anyone driving alongside a hot rod can see the

FORD'S 1932 OPEN CARS: ROADSTERS, PHAETONS & CABRIOLETS

Jon Hall's black '32 Roadster has a five-piece removable hardtop that can be stowed in the car's trunk. He's taken the shape of the center hood hinge and allowed it to flow into the mid-point of the windshield and down onto the grille shell. Hall also added a body molding line that ties the windshield to the beltline.

CHAPTER FOUR

Jim Austin's '32 Ford Roadster rides on cream-colored steel wheels that contrast nicely with the dark green body. The big selection of radial tires available today allow builders to dial in the perfect stance while retaining superior ride and handling qualities.

springs and shocks working as the car hits the slightest irregularity in the road. The only components on a hot rod are those that are needed to make it work. This minimalist approach makes viewing one on the highway a real treat, especially if you're hot rod builder Pete Chapouris. "One of the coolest days of my car life was when I was headed up to Santa Barbara, driving up the 101 highway in my coupe. It was one of those perfect days and way up in the distance I saw this black roadster. As I got close to it, I realized it was Doane Spencer's car. I didn't know at the time that Neal East had found it and put it back together. I came up behind that car in a 3/4 view and I about crapped. That car meant that much to me. I followed Neal at that position all the way up to Santa Barbara. It was unbelievable to see this hot rod icon out running. It was phenomenal!"

The 1932 Ford Roadster holds a unique place in American automotive history as an enduring symbol of hot rodding. Its appeal is universal. Anything that's well-designed is often hard to describe in words. Part of its charm is that a half-century ago these exceptionally well-styled cars sold for very little and could be easily modified. The 1932 Ford Roadsters were also very durable and looked great with or without fenders. The 1932 Ford Roadster will always be the quintessential American hot rod.

Right: *John Maynard's dark blue '32 Roadster has a slick set of headers sticking out of the engine compartment. Its stance is traditional hot rod with larger tires in the rear.*

FORD'S 1932 OPEN CARS: ROADSTERS, PHAETONS & CABRIOLETS

CHAPTER FIVE

1932 Ford Coupes

In 1932, Ford offered two distinctly different coupes: a three-window Deluxe model (shown here) and a five-window Standard. Both were available with Ford's dependable four-cylinder engine or the new V-8.

1932 FORD COUPES

Closed-body automobiles first appeared around 1905. Until that time all automobiles had been open roadsters and phaetons. The first closed cars offered a passenger compartment in the rear, leaving the driver exposed to the elements. Coupes (loosely defined as a closed passenger car with side-by-side seating for two) started to appear round 1910. By 1920, several car companies were offering closed coupes, but customers still preferred open touring cars. This preference for open cars may have been due in large part to the fact that the automobile was still a novelty. Cars were used for Sunday drives by those who could afford them. As cars became less expensive, they became more utilitarian. Consumers wanted something that could be driven in any climate and for a variety of purposes. Ford adapted quickly and added a coupe to its Model T line. Like most early coupes, this one looked more like a telephone booth on wheels than an automobile as we think of it today. The high roofs were for the convenience of those getting in or out and to accommodate the tall hats men wore at the time. All of these early coupes were a "five-window" design, with door glass and a smaller quarter window.

By the mid 1920s, the rooflines on the coupes were getting lower. While most of those built were of the five-window design, upscale landau coupes and three-window designs were starting to appear. When Ford released its Model A in 1928, an attractive five-window coupe was one of the body styles available. There were several stylish three-window coupes available in 1928, but most cost three times the price of Ford's coupe. While not as stylish as a three-window, the five-window design was more practical, giving the driver greater visibility. Ford offered a landau special coupe in its Model A line.

In 1932, Ford released two different Coupe models and one Sport Coupe variation. Ford's standard base coupe was the Model B-45 that featured a body built by Ford, Murray, or Briggs. It had five windows (but was listed in the sales material as a "four-window") and looked similar to the Model A coupe, with the exception of the missing shade over the windshield. Ford also released a special three-window Model B-520, but only in Deluxe trim. In Ford's 1932 sales material, the Victoria sedan is listed as a coupe. But today it is commonly called a sedan and will be treated as such in Chapter 6.

1932 Ford Sport Coupe

Ford based its 1932 Sport Coupe Model B-50 on the basic five-window body. The steel top portion was removed, along with the quarter windows and rear window, and replaced with a leather grain, fixed soft top with landau bars on the sides. The doors were identical to those on the five-window coupe. Ford broke from the convention of an all-metal body structure on the Sport Coupe's B-pillars and door headers. Instead, these were crafted out of wood and the sheet metal was nailed on. Ford also added drip rails over the doors, an unusual feature in a soft-topped car. Ford trimmed the inside of the soft top with a headlining material. The rear window could be zipped out for more ventilation or to talk to passengers riding in the rumble seat. Ford released the Sport Coupe as a special model and did not list it in the sales material as a Standard or Deluxe model. Its interior appointments were similar to those

The 1932 model year would be the last for Ford's Sport Coupe. Ford used the basic body structure of a five-window coupe, less the roof, to create the Sport Coupe. For its fixed soft top, Ford used a waterproof light brown landau grain material. The rear window unzipped, allowing conversations with passengers in the rumble seat. Ford did not offer a Deluxe version of the Sport Coupe.

103 ■ DEUCE: 75 YEARS OF THE '32 FORD

CHAPTER FIVE

This derelict Sport Coupe reveals the amount of wood Ford used in the construction of some of its 1932 Ford bodies. The B-pillar and door header structure are all wood on this model. The three-window's unique instrument panel has been installed in this particular car.

in the Standard coupe, but it had the laminated glass that was only available as standard equipment on the Deluxe model (optional on all Standard models). Ford's 1932 Sport Coupe did not sell well. Only 2,911 units were produced. Due to these low sales figures, Ford dropped the Sport Coupe model for 1933. Hot rodders have generally shied away from the Sport Coupe, mainly because of its fixed windshield posts and a fabric top that couldn't be folded down. One notable exception is the Jackman Brothers' highly chromed show car of the 1960s.

1932 Ford Five-Window Coupe

Ford offered its new five-window coupe for 1932 only as a Standard model. As a base model it featured few standard amenities. These included a dome light and sun

Even though Ford relegated the five-window to Standard status, it looks elegant enough to take a well-dressed couple to a trendy restaurant. It's easy to identify this car as one of the early production models by its 20-louver hood.

104 ■ DEUCE: 75 YEARS OF THE '32 FORD

1932 FORD COUPES

Ford's five-window coupe for 1932 only came in Standard trim. This older restoration is painted Washington Blue. To be a completely accurate restoration, the windshield frame should be painted body color instead of black.

visors similar to those offered on other Ford closed cars for 1932. Ford included one nice standard feature on the five-window—a roll down rear window. This gave the occupants a great deal of extra ventilation and, if equipped with the optional rumble seat, allowed conversation between driver and passengers. Ford also added a standard pull-down curtain for the rear window.

Designers installed a comfortable bench seat in the Standard coupe and covered it with either Thorn Brown mohair or Brown Diagonal Dash cloth upholstery material. At the beginning of the model year, Ford offered a genuine leather Copra Drab Fine Grain trim option for the five-window coupe, but this high-quality material was later dropped in favor of an artificial leather trim.

105 ■ DEUCE: 75 YEARS OF THE '32 FORD

Even though it was a Standard model, Ford added several nice amenities to its five-window coupe. The rear window could be rolled down. Ford also installed a dome light, rear window shade, and interior sun visors.

A rear luggage compartment was standard on the 1932 Ford five-window coupe. Ford used hidden hinges at the top and a single, lockable handle at the bottom. A rumble seat was an option and it used the same lid with different hardware.

The base five-window coupe came with a standard luggage compartment, but a rumble seat was optional. Ford trimmed the rumble seat with black-brown Fine Grain Colonial Grain artificial leather on cars trimmed with one of the cloth interiors. The early cars with genuine leather had the rumble seats trimmed in the same Copra Drab Fine Grain leather. Ford added a carpet for the rumble seat floor on the early production cars, but later changed to the same tan-colored rubber mat floor covering as the coupe's interior. Ford did not offer carpeting in the interior of the five-window coupe as an option, perhaps to facilitate a sale at dealerships.

1932 FORD COUPES

This particular V-8 powered five-window coupe can be identified as a later production model by its 25-louver hood. Domestically, Ford produced 31,112 V-8 powered five-window coupes.

At 27.8 inches, Ford's 1932 five-window coupe had one of the smallest door openings of all the models (the roadster was the smallest). Once inside, there was plenty of legroom and ample seating for two on a wide bench seat.

107 ■ DEUCE: 75 YEARS OF THE '32 FORD

CHAPTER FIVE

A rear-mounted spare tire was standard on Ford's five-window coupe. This one has a strap-style tire lock. Like all other 1932 Fords, the five-window was equipped with a single rear taillight mounted on the left-hand side.

1932 Ford Three-Window Coupe

To satisfy buyers who wanted a more upscale coupe, Ford released its Deluxe three-window coupe in April 1932—a month later than all other models. Three-window coupes had been positioned in the automobile market as being more exclusive and as having more standard amenities. The three-window design gave the body an elegant look over the more modest five-window versions. It offered a large door that hinged in the rear, opening "suicide" style. This was the first time Ford used a suicide door on any of its cars. It's also the only 1932 Ford with three door hinges. This larger door and its resultant swing made this the only model in Ford's 1932 lineup not to have the fender-mounted spare tire as an option because the tire would restrict the door from opening. The three-window coupe did not have a drip rail over the doors like all of Ford's other closed models. Instead, the roof had a lip than ran above the door opening. Ford's body engineers also added a small depression along the top of the inner door panel to channel any water out to the door's edges.

In addition to the unique doors, every other panel on the three-window body, with the exception of the cowl

108 ■ DEUCE: 75 YEARS OF THE '32 FORD

1932 FORD COUPES

Ford tried every trick in its bag to sell cars in the midst of a depression, including hiring celebrities to make personal appearances. Here legendary boxer Jack Dempsey poses in a new three-window coupe.

vent door, was unique and would not interchange with any other 1932 Ford model. Ford even added unique exterior door handles to the three-window. Ford chromed the three-window's windshield frame—the only closed Ford car in 1932 to have a chrome windshield frame. Even this windshield frame was unique and could not be used on any other Ford body. The three-window body was also longer than the other passenger car bodies. This length and the gentle curve of the rear body required the lower rear panel to be notched in the area of the gas tank filler. Like all other Deluxe models, Ford fitted the three-window coupe with cowl lamps and put laminated glass in all the windows.

Similar to the five-window coupe, the three-window came with a standard rear luggage compartment and a roll-down rear window. A rumble seat was optional. When equipped with a rumble seat, there was no exterior handle to open the rear compartment as on the five-window. Behind the seat back, Ford located a small knob near the rear window regulator handle to unlatch the rear compartment. This too was exclusive to the 1932 Ford three-window coupe.

The 1932 Ford Deluxe three-window coupe was Ford's first car with suicide (rear hinged) front doors. Ford did not fit the three-window with rain gutters above the doors. They did add a small lip to the roof and a channel on the top of the door's inner panel to channel water away. It was also the only closed car in Ford's 1932 lineup with a chrome windshield frame. Like almost everything else on this body, this frame would not interchange with any other Ford model.

The 1932 model year brought Fords first three-window coupe. This stylish car was only offered as a Deluxe model.

CHAPTER FIVE

Because of the three-window's unique door swing, Ford limited the spare tire to a rear-mount only. This coupe is fitted with a long list of accessories including a chrome spare tire cover, a spare tire lock, a right hand accessory taillight, white sidewall tires, and chrome trim rings. The color of this coupe is Winterleaf Brown Dark.

As a Deluxe model, the 1932 three-window coupe featured a finely trimmed interior with several options for seat coverings. Ford used three cloth combinations for the seating on the three-window coupe: Rose Beige Mohair, Brown Bedford Cord, and Tan Pinstripe. Initially, Copra Drab genuine leather was one of the available interior choices, but in July, Ford made it an extra-cost option. All 1932 Ford three-window coupes were equipped with door armrests. Closed Deluxe sedans were the only other cars in which Ford included armrests on its 1932 models, for the rear seats only.

Another feature seen only on the three-window coupe was an assist loop on the inner door trim panel to help passengers close the large door. The instrument panel contained the same oval shaped opening for the gauge insert, but featured an integrated ashtray on the passenger side. Ford designers made the door for the glove box trapezoidal in shape. To keep the instrument panel symmetrical, they created a similarly shaped raised panel on the driver's side. This unique instrument panel was only used in the three-window coupe. Like all other Deluxe models, Ford added a wood grain finish to the instrument panel and window garnish moldings. On the early production cars Ford used a Walnut Grain but soon after switched to a Plain Mahogany Grain. And the

1932 FORD COUPES

A rumble seat was an option on the three-window coupe. Three-window coupes so equipped did not have an external handle to open the rumble seat like all of Ford's other '32 models. Ford provided a small handle just behind the package tray to unlatch the compartment. Ford upholstered the three-window's rumble seat with an artificial leather. This unrestored coupe has the original material in place.

The A-pillar on Ford's three-window coupe did not blend into the beltline body molding like it did on all of Ford's other closed cars. The exterior door handles on the three-window were unique to that model. Also, the location of the exterior handle was below the body belt molding, again unique to Ford's three-window. Because it was a Deluxe model, all 1932 three-window coupes were equipped with cowl lights.

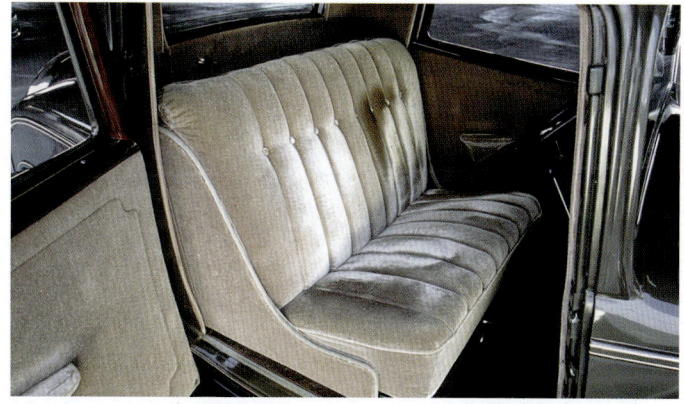

The door on Ford's 1932 three-window coupe was the largest of any model and was rear-hinged for effortless access to the plush interior. This coupe is upholstered in Rose Beige Mohair, but genuine leather and two other luxury cloth interiors were available. The three-window coupe's seat was the only one fitted with buttons.

111 ■ DEUCE: 75 YEARS OF THE '32 FORD

CHAPTER FIVE

The instrument panel on Ford's three-window coupe was unique and offered a glove box on the right side. Like all other Deluxe models, the three-window's instrument panel and window garnish moldings featured a wood-grained finish. The brown tapestry carpeting in this coupe is the same as the carpeting added to all closed Deluxe models.

window garnish moldings were of a unique design only seen on the three-window coupe.

1932 Ford Five-Window Hot Rods

The car that reset hot rodding's clock had to be the yellow 1932 five-window coupe in the movie *American Graffiti*. When that movie was released in 1972, interest in automobiles was waning. Muscle cars were on a morphine drip because of high insurance costs and looming emissions legislation. In the late 1960s and early 1970s, hot rods had taken a back seat to muscle cars, custom vans, and modified Volkswagens. High gas prices and long lines at the pump made a lot of people rethink the car hobby. Then along came a low-budget movie about cruising, starring a yellow deuce coupe. With this movie, people realized what a great era the 1950s and early 1960s had been, and how uninspiring VWs and vans were in comparison to hot rods. People also discovered that building a hot rod was more fun than going to the dealership to buy the latest muscle car in the hottest color. While hot rods were fast, you didn't have to drive fast to enjoy them. Cruising the main street in a five-window hot rod coupe at a slow speed with one's left arm on the windowsill, Milner-style, was a thrill in itself. It was as much about attitude as going fast. This is what *American Graffiti* gave to the American audience and to the phenomenon of hot rodding.

When George Lucas formulated *American Graffiti* in his mind, he saw the yellow coupe as its centerpiece. "Where were you in '62?" was the question asked in the promotional material for *American Graffiti*. Lucas wanted to put the American audience on the main street of a central valley California town in the early 1960s. Few imagined that this low-budget movie would end up as

Domestically, Ford built a total of 22,148 three-window coupes; 21,178 were equipped with a V-8 and only 970 were built with the four-cylinder engine. Like all other Deluxe models, safety glass was used in all windows.

1932 FORD COUPES

In the early 1970s, the insurance industry had sucked the oxygen out of the muscle car era's lungs. Emission controls and added safety equipment made new cars more expensive and less attractive. Then along came American Graffiti, *a low-budget movie about cruising. The star car was a chopped '32 coupe, and once again hot rodding flourished.*

one of America's landmark films. America's cruising culture, a yellow five-window coupe, and a number of unknown actors would soon be stars.

Producer Gary Kurtz and director George Lucas were both active in selecting the cars to represent the era.

Milner's five-window coupe was found in the Los Angeles area and purchased for $1,300. More than ten cars were considered, but this one caught the producer's eye because of its chopped top. When purchased, it had a full set of fenders. Like any aspiring starlet, it needed a

113 ■ DEUCE: 75 YEARS OF THE '32 FORD

The engine in Milner's coupe was a 327 Chevy with a Man-A-Fre intake manifold. The exhaust headers were sprint-car style.

1932 FORD COUPES

The yellow five-window coupe from American Graffiti *was originally purchased in Los Angeles for $1,300. The rear fenders were bobbed and motorcycle fenders were added to the front. Prior to filming it was painted an exceptionally bright yellow, because almost all of the filming would be done at night and the car had to appear vivid to show well on film.*

little plastic surgery for its screen test. Transportation manager Henry Travers had the task of producing the finished product and took it to a shop in Ignacio, California, where Bob Hamilton modified the car. Lucas wanted bobbed rear fenders, motorcycle front fenders, and a chopped grille shell. They stripped the coupe of several coats of paint and a fresh coat of Canary Yellow lacquer was added. Almost all of the filming was to be done at night and the coupe had to be exceptionally bright to show well on film. The coupe's dropped '32 front axle and 1940 Ford brakes were chrome plated. Hamilton added 14-inch chrome reverse wheels and a new set of tires.

Years earlier the coupe had been converted to Chevy power. For the movie, a freshly rebuilt 327 engine was added along with a T-10 four-speed transmission. They topped the engine with a Man-A-Fre intake with four Rochester two-barrel carburetors. Lucas also wanted a set of chrome sprint car-style headers, which were built by Johnny Franklin of Santa Rosa, California. For more acceleration, a set of 4.11 gears was added to the car's 1957 Chevrolet rear end.

Additional changes were made to the car for the magic of movies. The coupe's original red and white pleated interior was dyed black and a pocket was added to the right door for the "ticket" scene. Preparing a car for the movies means adding brackets for the attachment of

CHAPTER FIVE

The rear of the coupe that John Milner drove is fitted with a simple nerf bar and '48 Chevrolet taillights. The license plate, THX 138, refers to a prior George Lucas movie.

The interior of the five-window coupe that John Milner drove in American Graffiti *was originally red and white. It was dyed black for the movie and a pocket was added to the passenger side door. Because very little of the interior was seen during the movie, it received very little attention.*

Following the completion of the movie, Universal Studios tried to sell the coupe, but no one stepped up to buy it. It was refurbished for the sequel, More American Graffiti, *and then sold. Rick Figari of San Francisco currently owns the coupe. Figari has resisted the trend of over-restoration and just fixed what's needed to be repaired. He shows it quite often and occasionally drives it.*

1932 FORD COUPES

Jim Austin's hot rod five-window looks as though it could have come right out of the Ford factory. The stock headlights are mounted on a dropped headlight bar. The windshield frame is painted the color of the body and the striping pattern is similar to the style on the original cars. But the chopped top and rake give it away as being pure hot rod.

removable platforms for cameras and crewmembers. They modified the coupe's frame with the addition of several fixtures that virtually disappear to the viewer because of the frame's black color.

Actor Paul LeMat, who played John Milner, the owner of the coupe, had to look like he had owned and driven the coupe all his life. The car had to look like an extension of him—a task he pulled off well. For the safety of the actor, Travers took over for LeMat in the final high-speed race scene.

Once the production crew wrapped the film, Universal Studios had no faith that it would be able to recoup its investment with this small movie. In an effort to recover some money, they put the coupe, and other cars from the movie, up for sale. They set a price of $1,500 for the coupe, but no one bought it. Universal parked the coupe on its

CHAPTER FIVE

You can always find something interesting when stopping in at So-Cal Speed Shop's Pomona location. This bare metal five-window coupe has been chopped and channeled and is powered by a vintage Hemi engine. Other subtle modifications are the raised rear wheel openings.

Michigan hot rodder Jon Hall proves that a simple chopped five-window coupe doesn't need to be elaborate to be beautiful. The Marine Blue color is understated and the unpretentious flathead engine is the perfect antidote to crate engine mania. Even the windshield frame is not chromed but painted silver.

There is something special about watching a hot rod like Jon Hall's five-window going down the freeway. In a modern car, all of the components are hidden away from view, making the car appear sterile. On a hot rod like this, everything is exposed as it's being driven, and everyone can see the suspension working up and down and the engine spinning its accessories. It's true industrial art.

118 ■ DEUCE: 75 YEARS OF THE '32 FORD

1932 FORD COUPES

The red and white paint scheme of the So-Cal Speed Shop has been applied to Bob Everet's chopped five-window coupe. All the accessory pieces of this original steel coupe have been crafted to look like they were made in the late 1940s. The stance is also impressive.

Inset: *Traditional-style hot rods demand that the owner leave all of the original hardware in place. This includes door handles, door hinges, the deck lid handle, and hood latches. Combining a traditional element, '39 Ford taillights, with careful placement, creates a pleasing look.*

The interior of Everet's So-Cal coupe is elegant, comfortable, and looks like it could have been done in the 1940s. The window garnish moldings have been chrome plated and the carpet is a wool tapestry similar to what Ford used in 1932 in its Deluxe models.

back lot where tourists on the studio's tour could view it. Universal dusted it off for detail shots of its engine and instrument panel in the televised hot rod classic, *The California Kid*. The success of *American Graffiti* made the executives at Universal Studios happy that nobody bought the coupe. They quickly planned a sequel, *More American Graffiti*, and cleaned up the coupe. This time the coupe played a bit part in the movie. *More American Graffiti* didn't strike the same chord as the original and the studio again put the car up for sale. "The Fastest thing in the Valley," as

119 ■ DEUCE: 75 YEARS OF THE '32 FORD

CHAPTER FIVE

While lakes racers initially ignored coupes, drag racers embraced them. This chopped and channeled five-window is sitting in the staging lanes at Detroit Dragway in the early 1960s. This coupe is running a small-block Chevy engine with six two-barrel carburetors. One unique feature is the filled and peaked grille shell.

Milner called it, was sold to Steve Fitch, who also owned the black '55 Chevy that Harrison Ford (in the role of bad boy Bob Falfa) drove in the original movie.

In 1985, Fitch sold the car to Rick Figari. Figari was only eight years old when he first saw the movie, but he was mesmerized by the coupe. When he took delivery, the coupe needed some work to make it roadworthy. Figari drove it frequently until he came to appreciate the full historical significance of the car. Figari then limited his driving and made the car available for shows across the nation. He has maintained it, but bravely refuses to restore it. The coupe still has its original rough edges.

The yellow '32 five-window from *American Graffiti* is probably the most recognizable hot rod in the world. Bought and built on a shoestring, it has spawned more clones than any other hot rod. It wasn't built to mimic the hot rods that proliferated the B movies of the 1950s. It had a look all its own that grew out of its simplicity and the producer's vision. Thankfully, it has been preserved in its original condition.

Opposite: *Rich Guasco is a legendary hot rodder who recently built this dazzling chopped five-window coupe. One of the unique aspects of this coupe is the lengthened hood with the curved 1933-style louvers.*

120 ■ DEUCE: 75 YEARS OF THE '32 FORD

1932 FORD COUPES

Inset: The purple exterior and white interior color scheme of Guasco's coupe is reminiscent of Joe Nitti's famous roadster. The cut-down 1940 Ford instrument panel and steering wheel are also nostalgic touches that work well in any '32 Ford.

121 ■ DEUCE: 75 YEARS OF THE '32 FORD

CHAPTER FIVE

1932 Ford Three-Window Hot Rods

In the hot-rodding world, coupes have always suffered because they were closed and were viewed as family cars. However, the long-held bias against coupes dissolved as drag racing flourished at race venues where coupes were given their own classes. Coupes also saw more popularity in the Midwest and on the East Coast, where closed cars had been more popular than roadsters. It was only natural that the world's most famous 1932 Ford three-window coupe would hail from the Midwest.

Clarence "Chili" Catallo grew up in Dearborn, Michigan, and was no doubt influenced by *Hot Rod* magazine and the cars that covered its pages. Little did he know that a '32 three-window coupe he would build would become an icon of hot rodding and be on the cover of *Hot Rod* magazine as well as a Beach Boys record album.

In 1956, fifteen-year-old Clarence Catallo worked at his parents' small grocery store in Allen Park, a blue-collar

The term "rat rod" has been applied to bare-bones nostalgic hot rods that are usually painted in primer and hastily assembled. If this five-window is a rat rod, it has to be the most elegant one ever built. Sam Davis owns this coupe and built it with the same basic components that hot rodders used in the late 1940s—nothing billet and very little chrome plating.

"Chili" Catallo's three-window coupe is one of the most recognized 1932 Fords in the hot rodding world. It was first featured on the cover of Hot Rod *magazine and then on the cover of a Beach Boys album. Catallo's coupe was the perfect blending of the custom and hot rod worlds.*

122 ■ DEUCE: 75 YEARS OF THE '32 FORD

1932 FORD COUPES

Both the Alexander brothers of Detroit and Los Angeles-based Barris had a hand in the creation of Catallo's coupe. The last major project was the chopped top that was done in Barris' shop.

suburb of Detroit. In a gas station across the street from the store, he found and bought a three-window coupe for $75. Because he didn't have a driver's license, he asked a friend to drive it home for him. By the time Catallo got his license, his coupe was ready for the street. Initially, the car was channeled six inches, painted dark blue, and powered by a carbureted Oldsmobile V-8. Catallo added whitewall tires (dual whites in front) on black wheels and no hubcaps. Catallo's only major modification to the body was the raised rear wheel opening line. This subtle touch allowed the body character line to follow the shape of the rear tire, creating a pleasing silhouette.

In the summer, Catallo drove the car to his job in Allen Park. That's where I first saw the car in 1958. I lived about a mile away and after school I would ride my bike up to the gas station where Catallo parked his coupe. This was the first real hot rod I had ever seen on the street. I studied every inch of that car. More than anything, I wanted the owner of this coupe to offer me a ride in it. Every little model hot rod I built in the basement of

123 ■ DEUCE: 75 YEARS OF THE '32 FORD

CHAPTER FIVE

Catallo displayed his coupe at many of the major indoor auto shows. This is how it was displayed at Detroit's Autorama in 1962—a homecoming of sorts.

my house was influenced by Catallo's coupe. And when it came time to build a real '32 coupe, I looked to that car for inspiration.

Catallo took his coupe to the newly opened Detroit Dragway and turned the quarter in 12.9 seconds at 112 miles per hour. But like all hot rods, Catallo constantly improved his coupe. With each version, Catallo added more chrome and upgraded the engine. The three-carburetor intake soon made way for a McCullough blower. Silver scallops and white pinstripes were added to the body along with chrome wheels. This once-simple hot rod coupe was starting to flex its muscles.

In 1959, Catallo, who had picked up the nickname of "Chili," took the car to the Alexander Brothers, two of Detroit's top customizers. They sectioned the channeled body and added three horizontal wings to each frame rail. They fabricated a custom nose with vertically stacked quad headlights, and reworked the rear of the body with a rolled pan that matched the grille. Chrome exhaust stacks that ended at the leading edge of the frame rail wings were added to the Olds engine, along with six two-barrel carburetors. The chrome wheels were replaced by 1957 Plymouth hubcaps with white plastic flippers. The interior and top insert were trimmed in

Opposite: *Catallo's coupe constantly evolved during his ownership. It started out as a street-driven coupe, was drag raced, and then it morphed into a cutting edge show car. The deep channel of the body left little room for seat cushions.*

white Naugahyde with blue buttons. The Alexander Brothers added their trademark pair of dual recessed antennas with a small ridge in between on the left quarter panel. These antennas doubled as the switches for the electric door solenoids. *Silver Sapphire* became the name of Catallo's coupe. This Michigan car was ahead of its time and even several steps ahead of California's hot rods. Hot rods were supposed to be hot rods and not custom cars. Catallo and the Alexander brothers pushed the limits of hot rod design with this landmark coupe.

In 1960, the magnetic pull of the West Coast hot rod world was too much for Catallo to resist. He packed the *Silver Sapphire* and moved to California, where he took a job at George Barris' shop sweeping floors while he attended college. Not content with the car as it had been styled, he decided to make a few more major changes to the car. Barris chopped the top three inches and world-class painter Junior Conway added several coats of pearl Oriental Blue with white scallops in a pattern similar to the silver ones. Chrome wheels replaced the Plymouth hubcaps, but the whitewalls remained in place. The final touch was the addition of a chrome-plated GMC 671 blower and three Stromberg carburetors. The results

In the late 1950s a popular addition to a hot rod was a modern day steering wheel. Catallo selected this attractive wheel from a 1959 Lincoln Continental. He even used the windshield header to mount gauges.

124 ■ DEUCE: 75 YEARS OF THE '32 FORD

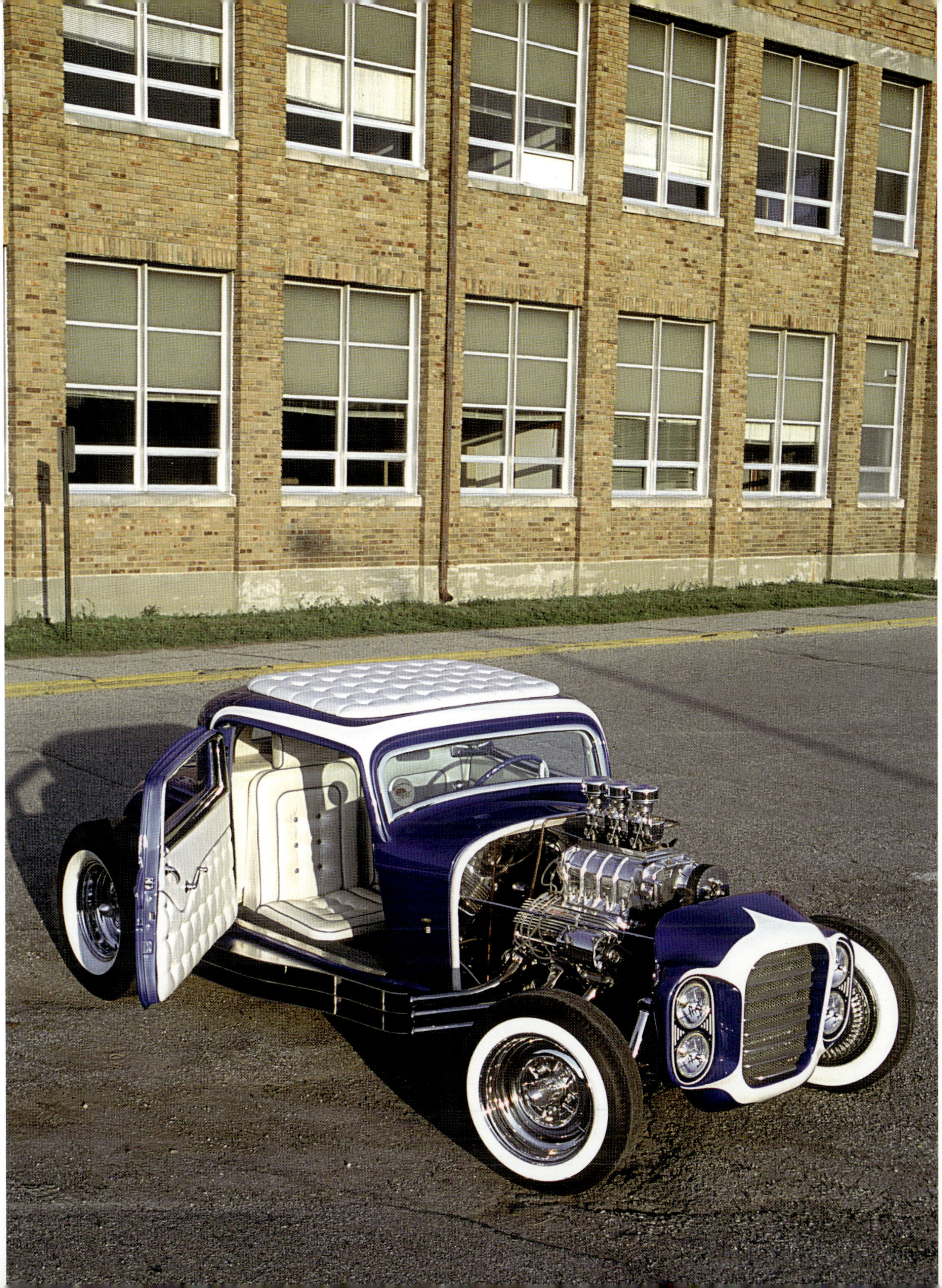

CHAPTER FIVE

were magnificent. Catallo's coupe was trendy for 1961, but it still retained the qualities of a traditional hot rod.

Soon after the work was complete, *Hot Rod* editor Bob Greene sent Eric Rickman to photograph Catallo's coupe. The images from that photo shoot ended up in a four-page spread in the magazine and on the cover. At that time the Beach Boys were riding the crest of a musical wave. When Capitol Records was about to release another Beach Boys album, they needed a hot rod coupe for the cover. George Barris suggested Catallo's coupe. The shot used was one of Rickman's outtakes from the *Hot Rod* shoot. Shortly after the album's release, Catallo sold his coupe. He had done everything possible to the car.

A Pennsylvania car club bought the coupe and showed it in several major car shows. It then went to a buyer in Montreal, Canada, and then to Ray Woloszak of Long Island, New York. Woloszak replaced the Olds engine with a Mopar 440 engine and then made a few changes to make the coupe street-worthy and drove it. Amazingly, the car remained basically intact for 30 years. Anything Woloszak removed from the car he kept. But after 32 years of ownership, Woloszak sold the car in 1999. Through a deal brokered by auto show promoter Bob Larivee, Chili Catallo bought back his coupe.

Catallo was determined to restore it to the way it looked on the cover of *Hot Rod* magazine. Unfortunately, shortly after starting the restoration, Catallo succumbed to a heart attack at age 58. His son Curt was determined to finish the project to honor his father. Using his Dad's gigantic scrapbook as a reference guide, he was able to restore the coupe to its original glory. In 2000, it was with great pride that the younger Catallo drove the coupe out onto the lawn at the Meadowbrook Concours d'Elegance. The hometown favorite won the People's Choice award. The coupe has gone on to be displayed at the Pebble Beach Concours and at the prestigious Petersen Automotive Museum in Los Angeles, California.

In 2003, I went to Clarkston, Michigan, to meet Curt Catallo and to photograph his dad's coupe for *Hot Rod Milestones*, a book written by Ken Gross for which I did the photography. For a location, I found an old high school not too far from where the coupe was stored. Once Curt got the car fired up and rolled it out of the garage, he looked up at me and said, "You want to ride with me?" It was a question I had waited 45 years to hear.

When Catallo first built his coupe he installed an Olds engine with tri-power. As the car continued to develop, he constantly upgraded the engine with more chrome and more power-boosting accessories. In its final state, it was equipped with a GMC blower topped with three chrome Stromberg 97s.

126 ■ DEUCE: 75 YEARS OF THE '32 FORD

1932 FORD COUPES

The Doyle Gammel Three-Window Coupe

The Doyle Gammel three-window is an example of a famous 1932 Ford coupe that ran with both fenders and a hood. It was featured in a 1963 issue of *Rod & Custom* magazine (photographed by Andy Southard) shortly after Gammel had purchased the car from Dick Bergren. Bergren had purchased it just a year earlier. And it was a young Bergren who took the saw to the coupe in his garage and gave it its famous top chop. He'd never chopped a car before and little did he know that his chop on this coupe would be its signature feature.

Chopping the top on a 1932 Ford coupe is like taking a section out of a funnel. Ford originally laid the windshield posts back on all 1932 Fords at a 10-degree angle. The C-pillars also have a slight taper as they go up. Most people who chop 1932 Fords will make a cut across the top at about the middle of the door, align the front A-pillars, and then align the C-pillars. This effectively pulls the front section forward and the rear section slightly rearward. This leaves a gap where the diagonal cut was made. A section is then added to lengthen the top. Bergren fought conventional wisdom and leaned back the A-pillars. Bergren claims he learned to chop a top by reading

Another vintage hot rod that left a big footprint on hot rodding's landscape is the Doyle Gammel coupe. This three-window was built in the early 1960s and was featured in Rod & Custom *magazine. It's now owned by Bruce Meyer and in true Bruce Meyer style, he's had it restored to its original grandeur by Bob Bauder.*

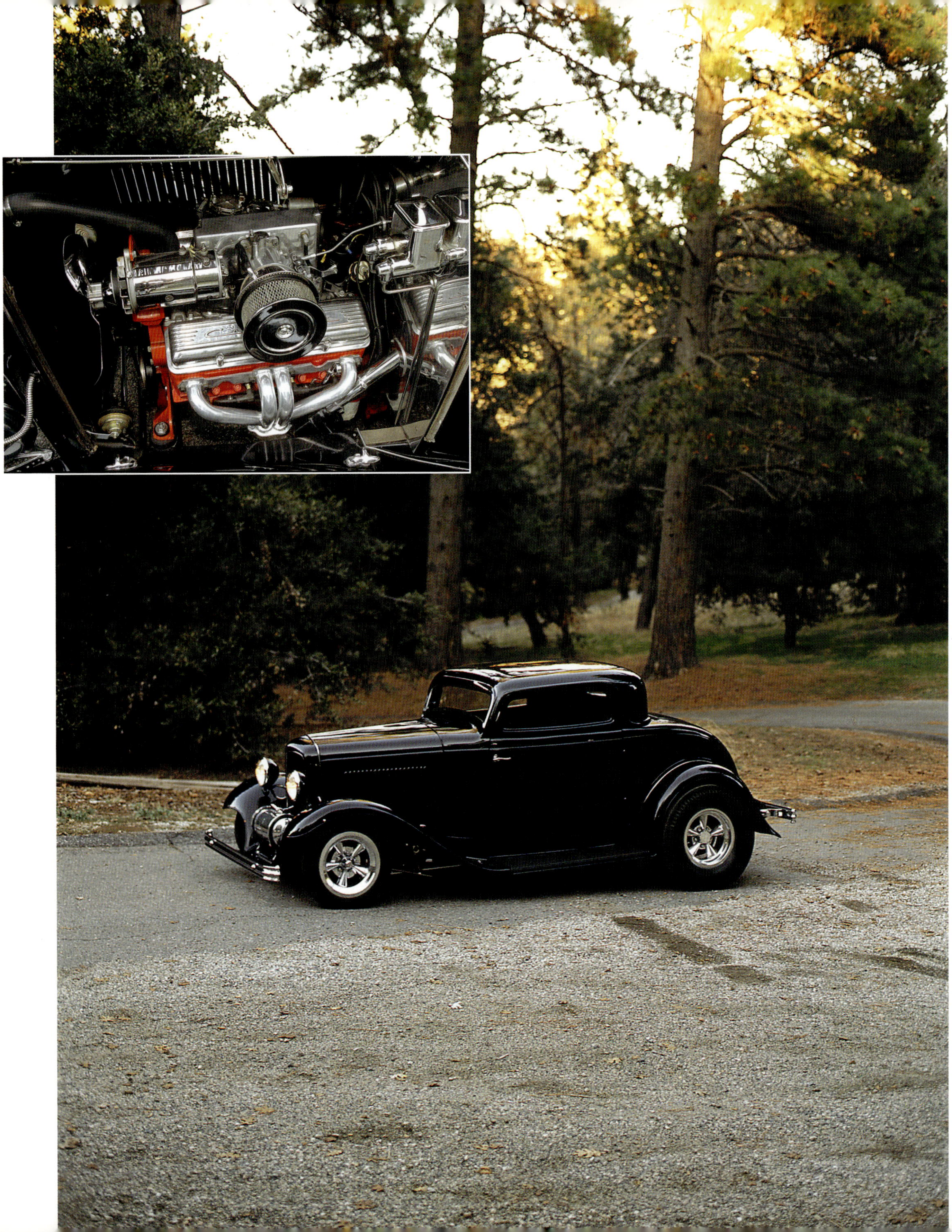

1932 FORD COUPES

Left: *Slanted A-pillars are a highly identifiable feature of the Gammel coupe. Laying the A-pillars back is not the traditional method of chopping a '32 Coupe, but it was done so well on this coupe that it became its fingerprint for identification.*

Left, Inset: *In the early 1960s, the hottest setup out of the factory was Chevrolet's Rochester fuel injection. In addition to adding outstanding performance, it looked futuristic in an era of simple carburetors. The polished aluminum firewall is another feature of cars built in the early 1960s.*

how to do it in a magazine. He had a little help from a friend who worked at a body shop. They also filled the opening in the roof and freely applied lead to smooth out the seams. Following the bodywork, Bergren took the coupe to a body shop for a few coats of dark root beer lacquer.

While in Bergren's short custody, other changes were made to the coupe that became associated with Gammel. Because he liked the looks of the Moon tank

With its column-mounted Sun tach and swizzle stick shifter, the interior of the Gammel coupe reflects the factory influence of the early 1960s Chevrolet cars. The instrument panel is a stock three-window coupe item with a custom gauge insert.

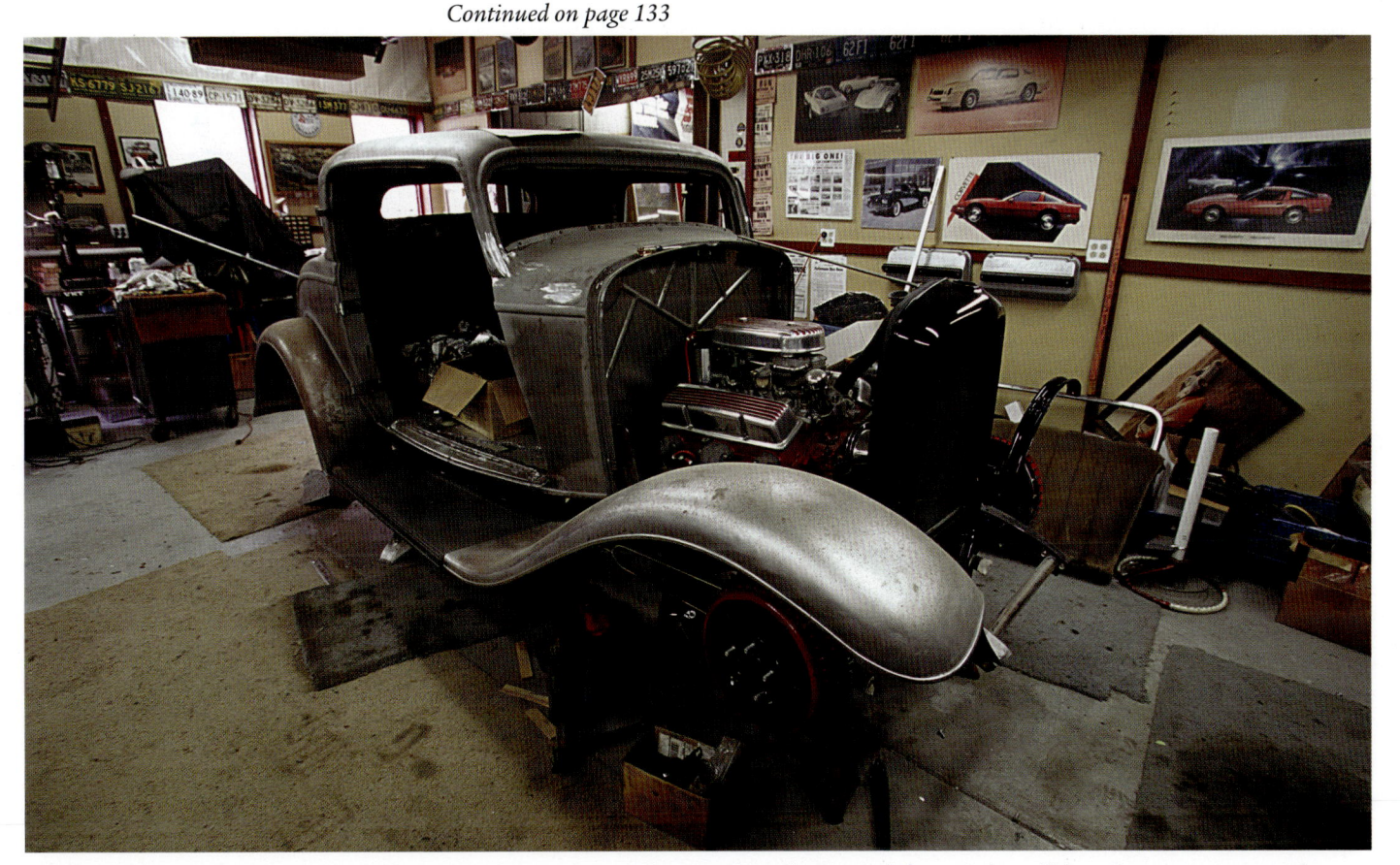

Continued on page 133

Plenty of '32 Fords are still built in small garages across America. When complete, this chopped three-window will have the same essence as the Gammel coupe with its chopped top, original fenders, and vintage small-block Chevy engine.

129 ■ DEUCE: 75 YEARS OF THE '32 FORD

Top 75 1932 Ford Hot Rods

In 2005, Ford Motor Company recognized that the 75th anniversary of the 1932 Ford was just around the corner. As part of the celebration to take place in 2007, they formed a blue ribbon committee of hot rod journalists and historians to select the top seventy-five 1932 Ford hot rods of all time. In a letter to committee members Edsel Ford, great grandson of Henry Ford, wrote:

"The 1932 Ford was a watershed vehicle for Ford, for the industry, and for American culture. With the first mass-produced V-8 engine and styling that is still genuine, honest and handsome, the '32 was the perfect combination of Henry Ford's engineering innovation and his son Edsel's styling sophistication. Seventy-five years later, these two qualities continue to be at the core of our business.

"The '32 Ford played a major role in another automotive revolution—the hot rod. Made from castoff cars, built in backyards and incorporating ingenuity and intuitive engineering, these simple machines performed far beyond their original capabilities, often rivaling the best in the world. This uniquely American form of automotive expression changed motor sports and became the foundation of the aftermarket industry. The hot rod is now an international symbol of originality, youth, and fun."

Here is the list of the 75 cars selected:

- **American Graffiti** – 5-window
- **Boyce Asquith** – Roadster
- **Lloyd Bakan** – 3-window
- **Balchowsky/Vogel** – Roadster
- **Banker Bros.** – 3-window
- **Gray Baskerville** – Roadster
- **Jeff Beck** – 3-window
- **Berardini Bros.** – Roadster
- **Bill Breece** – 3-window
- **Andy Brizio** – Roadster
- **Roy Brizio** – Roadster
- **Ray Brown** – Roadster
- **Brian Burnett** – Roadster
- **Lil' John Buttera** – 3-window
- **C&T Automotive/Siroonian** – Roadster
- **Clarence "Chili" Catallo** – "Little Deuce Coupe"
- **Pete Chapouris** – "Limefire" Roadster
- **Boyd Coddington** – Boydster I
- **Li'l Coffin** – Sedan
- **Phil Cool** – Roadster
- **Currie Enterprises** – Roadster
- **Bill Desatoff** – 2-door
- **Roy Desbrow** – Pick-up
- **Neal East** – Roadster
- **Neal East** – 5-window

- **Eastwood & Barakat** – 2-door
- **Vic Edelbrock, Sr.** – Roadster
- **Ells /Hansen** – Roadster
- **Dan Fink** – "Speedwagon"
- **Fjastad/Von Hofgaarden** – 2-door
- **Tommy Foster** – Roadster
- **Doyle Gammell** – 3-window
- **Richard Graves** – Phaeton
- **Ken Gross** – Roadster
- **Guldahl /Henderson** – Roadster
- **Wayne Henderson** – Vicky
- **Herbert /Gaskin** – 4-door
- **Ermie Immerso** – Roadster
- **Jackman Bros.** – Sport Coupe
- **Andy Kassa** – 3-window
- **Kendrick /Beck** – 2-door
- **Gary Kessler** – Roadster
- **Jim Khougaz** – Roadster
- **Bob Kolmos** – Phaeton
- **Jerry Kugel** – Roadster
- **Jerry Kugel** – Roadster - Bonneville
- **Dennis Kyle** – Roadster
- **Tony La Masa** – Roadster
- **Lobeck/Bauder/Coonan/Meyer** – Roadster
- **Harry Luzader** – 5-window

- **Dave Marquez** – Roadster
- **Mike Martin** – 3-window
- **McGee/Scritchfield** – Roadster
- **Tom McMullen** – Roadster
- **Bruce Meyer** – 3-window
- **Ak Miller** – Roadster
- **Bob Morris** – Roadster
- **Joe Nitti** – Roadster
- **Orange Crate** – Sedan
- **Veda Orr** – Roadster
- **Chuck Price** – Roadster
- **Tom Prufer** – 3-window
- **Roger Ritzow** – Roadster
- **Bob Rothenberg** – Roadster
- **Dick Scritchfield** – Phaeton
- **George Sein** – 5-window
- **John Siroonian** – Phaeton
- **Doane Spencer** – Roadster
- **Fred Steele** – Roadster
- **Ed "Axle" Stewart** – Roadster
- **Don Thelen** – Vicky
- **Don Van Hoff** – 5-window
- **Walsh/Walsh/Cusack** – Roadster
- **Tony Waters** – Roadster
- **Lynn Yakel** – 5-window

1932 FORD COUPES

The late Gray Baskerville's red, full-fendered roadster (currently owned by Jim Shelton) was the only car selected by every member of the committee to be named as one of the top 75 1932 Ford hot rods. Baskerville, one of hot rodding's preeminent journalists, drove this car on a regular basis, and the car was a reflection of him as an individual. (Photo courtesy Kevin Lee)

CHAPTER FIVE

Full-fendered and chopped '32 three-window coupes, such as this one owned by David Boule, look great with the right-size tires and correct stance. The wide whitewall tires mounted on chrome wheels give this coupe a real '50s look.

132 ■ DEUCE: 75 YEARS OF THE '32 FORD

1932 FORD COUPES

Gammel replaced the 265 Chevy with a bored-out 283. Along the way he installed a hot roller cam and recalibrated the fuel injection. The coupe could run the quarter-mile in 13.10 seconds at a speed of 99 miles per hour. While in Gammel's custody, Ed Roth pinstriped it for him. But like Bergren, he didn't keep the car for very long.

Bob Porter bought the coupe from Gammel for $1,900. He set about making several changes to the car including a new suspension and a big-block Chevy. Porter liked life in the fast lane, so fast that he ended up doing time and died young. During the time he owned it, some other unseemly characters who had a grudge against Porter damaged the coupe's body. With Porter out of the picture, the car bounced around from shop to shop with its title in limbo. Finally a Temple City, California, motorcycle dealer, Dick Weaver, sorted things out and acquired the car. Weaver had the body repaired and applied another coat of root beer brown paint. After a few years of ownership, Weaver sold it to Stan Van Amburgh, who quickly turned it over to Tom Schiffilea. Of the many changes Schiffilea made to the coupe, the most prominent has to be the bright purple paint with flames.

The grille shell on Boule's three-window coupe has been filled and given a slight peak. Small details like this make for outstanding hot rods.

on the front of Tom McMullen's roadster, Bergren added one to the coupe. He also added a set of five-spoke American mag wheels.

With the exterior set, Bergren looked under the hood. Before he bought the car, the previous owner had installed a 265 cubic inch Chevy engine backed by a Cad/LaSalle transmission. In 1962, Corvettes with Rochester fuel injection were the hottest thing on the street. Bergren bought a new fuel injection unit and installed it on the coupe's small-block Chevy. These units have traditionally been temperamental and difficult to dial in. But the mechanics at Los Angeles' biggest Corvette dealer, Harry Mann Chevrolet, had the expertise to get the most out of the exotic unit. Bergren also added 1957 Corvette fuel injection emblems to the hood sides. Bergren traded the Cad/LaSalle stick transmission for an Olds Hydramatic transmission. The last thing he did under the hood was to add an aluminum firewall. These represent quite a few changes to a car he had only owned for a short time. But these changes gave this coupe a unique signature that would follow it all its life.

This photo of a '32 three-window coupe was shot in the late 1940s. The chopped top has laid-back A-pillars similar to the Gammel coupe. The grille shell is missing and the engine looks like an original '32 V-8 with a Jack Henry dual carburetor manifold added.

CHAPTER FIVE

This modern-day hot rod looks as if it could have been built on the 1940s. It's been chopped and channeled and the little flathead engine has a vintage two-carb manifold that is tall enough to let the carburetors edge above the height of the cowl.

1932 FORD COUPES

This steel gray '32 three-window has just completed its burnout and is about to stage. Its body is completely stock, right down to the cowl lights. But it's a wonder they stay attached because this coupe consistently runs the quarter at speeds over 120 miles per hour.

Even with this long line of owners, the coupe still had many of its original identifying markers—the most prominent being the boldly chopped top. With the bones still intact, all it needed was a new owner who would honor its heritage. Up stepped hot rod collector Bruce Meyer. Meyer started buying vintage racecars and hot rods long before it became fashionable, or profitable. He loves three-window coupes, especially this one because of the way the roof had been chopped. Meyer turned it over to hot rod builder/restorer Bob Bauder, who restored its essence.

When Bauder took the car apart he found that the years and excessive horsepower and hard driving had taken their toll. He removed the big-block Chevy engine that had been installed several owners ago. Bauder also took the suspension back to its original hot rod buggy springs and added a 1956 Ford pickup steering gear. The exterior reflects the Gammel look: brown root beer paint, American mag wheels, and fuel injection emblems on the side of the hood. Under the hood is a 283 cubic inch engine that has been bored 1/8-inch with a vintage Rochester fuel injection unit on top. Behind the engine is a fresh sheet of polished aluminum that replaced the one that Bergren had installed decades earlier. Bauder successfully turned back the clock on this historic three-window.

The individuals who own the three hot rod coupes in this chapter have a passion for hot rodding and a connection to their cars' history. These cars were not bought or restored as investments, but out of a sense of capturing that short tick of the clock when these cars were celebrated in the movies or on the pages of hot rod magazines. Fame would not have come about had these coupes lacked the hot rod chops to begin with.

Henry Ford took a bold step when he introduced two different coupes in 1932. Engineers could just as easily have upgraded the five-window with the Deluxe trim package and saved a lot of money; instead, they created a one-of-a-kind classic with the three-window coupe. Once hot rodders got over their roadster addiction, they saw that both of Ford's coupes could be made into impressive hot rods. Chopping the top improved the proportions on the coupes in the same way it did on the roadsters. And all of the traditional hop up techniques worked equally as well on a coupe as on a roadster.

CHAPTER SIX

Ford's 1932 Sedans and Commercial Vehicles

Ford's best-selling model in 1932, at 124,101 domestic units, was its two-door sedan. This unrestored Standard model was originally optioned with a V-8 engine and Apple Green wheels. The World War II gas rationing stickers are still in the windshield.

136 ■ DEUCE: 75 YEARS OF THE '32 FORD

FORD'S 1932 SEDANS AND COMMERCIAL VEHICLES

Ford's sedan lineup was its bread and butter for 1932. Although they were not as sporty as roadsters or coupes, sedans provided plenty of comfort in an attractive package. The changing attitude toward ownership of a car could clearly be seen in the sales figures for sedans, which outsold coupes and roadsters by a high margin. The customer's perceived value of the sedans was high. Now the entire family could ride in comfort, completely protected from the elements.

Ford also made quite a few commercial vehicles in 1932. Some were based on the passenger car and others were unique models. Ford tried to have something for everyone in 1932 and its lineup of unique cars reflected that intention.

1932 Ford Two-Door Sedan

With total sales reaching 124,101 units, the two-door sedan (also known as the "Tudor") was Ford's best-selling passenger car in 1932. Standard models outsold Deluxe versions at a rate of four to one. Customers chose the new V-8 over the four-cylinder engine in the two-door sedans by a wide margin. In addition, the new body featured gentle curves that quickly made the boxy Model A sedans appear outdated.

Ford's two-door sedans were exceptionally roomy and well appointed. All two-door sedans were fitted with a pair of front bucket seats. Ford engineers hinged the front of the right hand seat so it could be tilted forward to allow passengers to access the rear seat more easily. At

This Standard Model B is typical of the many Ford sedans sold in 1932. Ford's all-steel body offered a superior structure compared to competitors that used wood as a structural element.

137 ■ DEUCE: 75 YEARS OF THE '32 FORD

CHAPTER SIX

17-3/4 inches, the rear seat on the two-door sedan offered more legroom than any of Ford's other models. Ford fitted all two-door sedans with a dome light, sun visors, rear carpeting, and a pull-down rear window shade. A wood grain instrument panel and window moldings, along with full carpeting, rear seat armrests, passenger assist loops, and rear seat ashtrays were added to the interior of the Deluxe sedan. Ford offered the same basic set of materials for the Standard and Deluxe sedans as they did for other models. Throughout the year, Ford added and deleted materials for Standard models. Genuine leather was an available trim choice for the Deluxe models and artificial leather trim could be specified for the Standard versions late in the model year. Body pinstripes were identical on the Standard and Deluxe models.

Ford's 1932 two-door sedans offered its rear seat passengers maximum legroom. The Deluxe versions included rear seat armrests and ashtrays. The right-hand passenger seat folded forward for access to the rear seat.

This young lady is about to enter a 1932 Ford Deluxe two-door sedan. The two-door offered wide door openings and a passenger seat that folded forward for access to the rear seat. All Deluxe models interiors were trimmed with high-quality materials.

138 ■ DEUCE: 75 YEARS OF THE '32 FORD

FORD'S 1932 SEDANS AND COMMERCIAL VEHICLES

1932 Ford Four-Door Sedan

Ford's 1932 four-door sedan (also known as a "Fordor") also sold well, with a total of 37,363 units. This was the only 1932 Ford body style that attracted more Deluxe customers than Standard buyers. The four-door also attracted more V-8 customers than buyers who wanted a four-cylinder engine. The interior of both the Standard and Deluxe four-door models followed the same treatments as the two-door. The most notable difference in the interior is the use of a front bench seat in the four-door sedan instead of bucket seats.

This is the interior of a 1932 Ford Deluxe two-door sedan. This was the first year that Ford added sun visors to the interiors of its closed cars. The instrument panel and window frames on all of its Deluxe sedans were finished with a wood-grained appearance.

Ford's 1932 four-door sedan offered the buyer the convenience of two extra doors with the style and elegance of a more expensive car. This is a Deluxe model that offered full safety glass and exterior cowl lamps.

139 ■ DEUCE: 75 YEARS OF THE '32 FORD

CHAPTER SIX

Inset: Ford's 1932 Deluxe four-door sedan offered rear seat passengers an armrest and ashtray. The small handle is used to raise and lower the small quarter window. This particular unrestored sedan is trimmed in its original Rose Beige mohair.

By today's automotive design standards this Deluxe four-door appears boxy, but in 1932 it featured the latest in design trends including a smooth grille shell and slanted A-pillars. The color combination is Tunis Gray with Old Chester Gray body moldings. The body's pinstriping and wheels are Tacoma Cream.

The 1932 Ford four-door sedan's body featured some unique components. The rear doors were hinged in the "suicide-style." Because the door swung rearward, it offered easy access for rear seat passengers, even though the door opening was small. Ford engineers designed the rear door so it would not hit the rear fender when open. The front doors on the four-door sedan appear similar in size to those used on the five-window coupe but in fact, they are unique to each model. Ford also built all of its 1932 four-door sedans with a quarter window that could be partially lowered.

FORD'S 1932 SEDANS AND COMMERCIAL VEHICLES

Ford included stronger rear springs for its sedan models to be able to carry the extra weight of rear seat passengers. This Deluxe four-door is equipped with an accessory spare tire cover.

The 1932 Ford Victoria Sedan

Ford offered its customers an additional sedan for 1932—the Victoria. The Victoria sedan, often listed as "Victoria Coupe," offered "Continental" styling with its unique bustle-back body. Its styling is reminiscent of the Weymann-built Stutz Monte Carlo or Reo Royale. Ford only offered this special two-door sedan as a Deluxe model with its full line of Deluxe interior and exterior appointments. Ford sold 8,580 Victorias in 1932 and 8,054 were V-8 models. Only 526 customers opted for the four-cylinder engine.

The Victoria was one of the few cars produced by Ford that used wood as a structural element in the construction of the body. A wood panel was used to mount the quarter window regulator. This may have been a practical approach to building automotive components that would be produced only in limited numbers.

The Victoria's doors appear identical to those on a two-door sedan, but they are not interchangeable. Unlike the Standard coupe and Sport Coupe, the doors on these two sedans are unique. Even the door glass is different. But the Victoria's doors were interchangeable with the B-400 Convertible Sedan. The design of the Victoria's body also took away 9 1/8 inches of rear legroom. The backrest on the rear seat could be pulled

Ford's Victoria sedan had a distinctive humped back evocative of the designs of some of Europe's most elegant sedans. All Victoria sedans were built as Deluxe models. The body color on this Victoria is Brewster Green light, with Brewster Green medium moldings. The stripe is Silver Gray and the wheels are Apple Green. This stylish sedan also features the accessory right-hand taillight and spare tire cover.

forward to access the limited storage area in the rear of the body.

Other than the unique European-styled body, it's amazing to see that Ford offered the Victoria sedan in 1932. It might have been smarter for Ford to offer its two-door sedan only in Standard trim and then have the

CHAPTER SIX

The interiors of the Victoria sedans were trimmed in elegant cloths, such as this striped broadcloth. Like the two-door sedan, the Victoria also featured front bucket seats. Ford engineers hinged the passenger seat at the front to allow easier access to the rear seat.

The rear seat of the Victoria offered the least amount of legroom of any of the 1932 Ford sedans. But what it lacked in legroom it more than made up in style. The floor was covered with wool carpeting and Ford added armrests and ashtrays for the passengers' convenience. All closed Ford cars were equipped with a rear window shade with a tassel added to the pull on Deluxe models.

FORD'S 1932 SEDANS AND COMMERCIAL VEHICLES

One of the most elegant colors for any 1932 Ford is Washington Blue. This Victoria's body moldings are painted black with a Tacoma Cream pinstripe and Tacoma Cream wheels. The side-mounted spare and white sidewall tires add a touch of upscale elegance. Ford sold a total of 8,580 Victoria models in 1932.

Victoria as the sole Deluxe two-door sedan, much like they did with the coupes. It appears as though Ford had two competing models for the same target market segment.

The 1932 Ford B-400 Convertible Sedan

Ford offered a two-door Convertible Sedan in 1932. More commonly known by its model number B-400, it is unusual because of its fixed side window frames and full folding top. All B-400s were Deluxe models. Sales of the B-400 were negligible with only 926 sold. With so few sales, 1932 would be the last year for this intriguing body style.

Like some of the other 1932 Ford "orphan" body styles, the B-400 contained many unique parts, some of which it shared with other body styles. It shared its passenger doors with the Victoria sedan, but not with the two-door sedan. The B-400's chrome windshield frame and cowl assembly are similar to the Cabriolet's. Its

CHAPTER SIX

This B-400 Convertible Sedan is one of 926 built and is an unrestored original. Until a few years ago, it was a daily driver. The B-400s were unique in the fact that they were the last convertible sedan model built by Ford and the first convertible sedan to be built with a V-8.

The top on this B-400 has been folded back and its "dust hood" has been added. Because of the low production, Ford used a lot of wood in this body to save money on its construction.

chrome rear window frame and laminated glass were also used on the Deluxe Roadster, Sport Coupe, and Deluxe Phaeton. Ford also made extensive use of wood in constructing this body. Ford used wood for the inner framework around the quarter windows and over the doors. Engineers also used wood for the inner quarter panel window regulator, similar to the Victoria sedan.

While coveted by collectors as the last convertible sedan built by Ford, and the only one with the V-8, the B-400 never caught on with hot rodders. Most likely, many were cannibalized for parts after the bodies had been

All B-400s were outfitted as Deluxe models. The doors on the B-400 were the same as those used on the Victoria sedans. The quarter panels were unique to this model and the internal framing structure around the door and quarter window was wood. The B-400 has been ignored by hot rodders but loved by restorers.

scrapped. Its reduced production numbers and partial wooden structure also are contributing factors to its scarcity today.

The 1932 Ford Sedan Delivery

With only 400 produced, the 1932 Ford Sedan Delivery is the most rare of the '32s. Ford based this model on its two-door sedan and it was the last body style to go into production. It carries the same body as a two-door sedan with the quarter windows filled and a third door added to the rear. This third door is hinged on the left and has a drip rail on the roof above the door opening. Ford removed the rear seat and added a flat wooden load floor that extended from the base of the door opening to the rear of the front seats. The rear door required moving the spare tire to the fender-well mount and adding a straight rear spreader bar. The stock passenger car fuel tank was used. Ford kept the two-door's front bucket seats, but only offered one interior trim combination in Copra Drab artificial leather. Ford retained the forward folding right-hand seat. Designers covered the front floor with a rubber mat and finished the sides of the rear storage area with brown painted Masonite. Even though it was a commercial vehicle, the Sedan Delivery was available in all standard colors that Ford offered in 1932. The pinstriping was done in the same pattern and colors as its two-door sedan. While some of Ford's other 1932 commercial vehicles used a unique grille shell, the Sedan Delivery used a standard passenger car grille and shell.

Ford created a custom rear door for the Sedan Delivery. Engineers built the structure out of wood and applied the sheet metal over it. It was most likely formed from the rear panel of a sedan. Ford installed three hinges on the rear door. The rear window on that door was fixed in place and the inner molding for the rear window was made of wood. The entire door framing on the rear of the body was also made of wood. It is obvious that the easiest way to get custom bodywork done in 1932 was to hire coachbuilders who knew how to make a body out of wood.

The 1932 Ford Sedan Delivery proved itself to be an effective commercial delivery vehicle for light loads, such as baked goods and flowers. The large side panel offered

Continued on page 148

With only 400 built, the rarest of any of the 1932 Ford body styles is the Sedan Delivery. Ford created this light-duty delivery vehicle out of a two-door sedan by removing the rear seat, adding a flat load floor, and a door at the rear. Because of the opening rear door, all Sedan Deliveries were equipped with a side-mounted spare. The pinstriping pattern on the Sedan Delivery is the same as the two-door sedan.

In the 1932 Sedan Delivery, Ford retained the standard two-door sedan front seats and added a wooden load floor that stretched from the rear door to the back of the front seats. The interior side panels and rear door inner panels were trimmed with Masonite.

FORD'S 1932 SEDANS AND COMMERCIAL VEHICLES

Julian Alvarez is the owner of this mildly hot-rodded Sedan Delivery. Ford simply added flat sheet metal panels to block out the quarter windows. The rear door is hung with three hinges.

CHAPTER SIX

plenty of space on which the owner could advertise his business. Ford retained the Sedan Delivery model for the redesigned 1933 model, this time basing the unique body on the four-door rather than a two-door sedan. Sales of the Sedan Delivery in 1933 totaled 3,666 units.

1932 Ford "Woody" Station Wagon

Station wagons were given their name because they were first designed to transport people and their luggage to and from the train station. Based on a passenger car chassis, these hand-built vehicles have become favorites of collectors. In 1929, Ford made the station wagon a regular production model. The 1932 Ford Station Wagon provided seating for eight people in its three rows of seats. Because of its commercial roots, Ford installed artificial leather trim on the seats and put a rubber mat on the floor. The extra length of the body and placement of the third row of seats made it necessary to place the fuel tank under the passenger's front seat.

The inner structure of the rear door on a Sedan Delivery is made of wood. Ford also used wood to create the garnish molding for the rear window. The exterior drip rail above the rear door is made out of sheet metal. Ford used nails to attach it to the wooden structure that surrounds the doorframe on the body. All Sedan Deliveries used a straight rear spreader bar.

Because of the low production numbers and a body unlike any other Ford manufactured, Ford turned to Baker-Raulang to create their Station Wagon model. The wood used for these cars came from a half-million acres Henry Ford owned in Michigan's Iron Mountain area. While cowl lamps were reserved for Deluxe models, they became a standard item on all Station Wagons built after August 1932.

148 ■ DEUCE: 75 YEARS OF THE '32 FORD

FORD'S 1932 SEDANS AND COMMERCIAL VEHICLES

Ford's 1932 Station Wagon provided seating for eight people in three rows of seats. Because of its intended use as a commercial vehicle, Ford installed Copra Drab Fine Grain Colonial artificial leather trim on the seats and a rubber floor mat.

The cost of making a limited production car, such as the station wagon, out of steel would have been too much to be practical. There were still plenty coach builders familiar with wooden construction who were willing to construct station wagons. All they needed was enough wood. Henry Ford solved that problem by purchasing a half-million acres of Michigan's Iron Mountain forest. This allowed Ford to dominate the station wagon market. Starting in 1929, Ford was the first auto manufacturer to mass-produce a station wagon on its own assembly lines. These Model A station wagon bodies were built by coachbuilders Murray, in Detroit, or Baker-Raulang, of Cleveland, Ohio. Baker-Raulang had a long history of coachbuilding and, in 1932, became the sole supplier of station wagon bodies to Ford Motor Company. Murray was too busy with other 1932 Ford bodies. Ford would ship its kiln-dried wood to subcontractor Mengel Body Company of Louisville, Kentucky; they, in turn, would construct sub-assemblies and ship them to Baker-Raulang.

The wooden body on Ford's 1932 Station Wagon looks somewhat boxy compared to the sleek all-steel bodies used

CHAPTER SIX

The extra length of the Station Wagon body prevented the addition of any rear bumpers. This length also required the elimination of the rear-mounted fuel tank and the addition of a fuel tank under the front passenger's seat.

on passenger cars. There were no well-executed curves in the wood body. But the varnished wooden body had amazing appeal due to its color, warmth, and texture, much like an elegant piece of furniture or classic wooden boat. Ford used birch plywood panels with solid maple framing on the exterior. Almost all of the wood used was "first cut" from Ford's vast Iron Mountain reserve. First-cut wood has a tighter grain structure and fewer knots than second-growth trees from the same land. Basswood roof slats supported the black top fabric on the interior. Spar varnish coated all of the wood. The only paint on the body was on the cowl, hood, and grille shell (the fenders and frame were black like all other 1932 Fords). Ford used three different shades of brown on the station wagons in 1932: Manila Brown until May, Winterleaf Brown from May to July, and Light Emperor Brown from July to the end of production. Unlike other 1932 Fords, there were no pinstripes on the station wagon. Most of the body hardware came from the bins filled with unused Model A parts. Even though there was no Deluxe version, cowl lamps were added as standard equipment to the station wagon in August 1932. Prior to that date they could be added as an accessory.

Baker-Raulang used birch plywood panels with solid maple framing on the exterior. All of the wood was beautifully varnished. The side curtains were constructed of tan fabric with clear plastic panels. They slid in channels that extended up to the roof.

150 ■ DEUCE: 75 YEARS OF THE '32 FORD

FORD'S 1932 SEDANS AND COMMERCIAL VEHICLES

Baker-Raulang attached this plate to each of the 1932 Ford Station Wagon bodies they built.

On some models, Ford used carry-over Model A components, such as these exterior door handles on the Station Wagon.

Left: *Baker-Raulang used standard angle iron for the framework of Ford's Station Wagon tailgate. The chains that support it in this position are covered with the same material as the top.*

Ford's 1932 Station Wagon was listed as a commercial vehicle, but was built with passenger car appointments. Early models, like the one in this photograph, did not have cowl lights. Three different shades of brown were used on station wagons during the model year, but pinstriping was never added.

151 ■ DEUCE: 75 YEARS OF THE '32 FORD

CHAPTER SIX

The tailgate on Ford's 1932 Station Wagon could be unlatched and folded horizontally. Each side window (there were three on each side) and the rear window were adorned with curtains. These curtains were made of a tan fabric frame around clear plastic windows. The side curtains slid up on tracks to the open position. In the full open position, they were stowed along the inside of the roof. The rear window curtain unsnapped from its fabric frame, folded along its upper edge, and snapped into its stowed position on the inside of the roof.

1932 Ford Pickups – Closed and Open

Ford offered a closed cab and a Roadster pickup in 1932. Both of these vehicles were built on a passenger car chassis with many "car-like" components, but were sold as commercial vehicles. The first pickup Ford released in 1932 was the closed-cab Model B-82. This was followed later in the year with the open-cab Roadster version B-76. Most pickups were equipped with a four-cylinder engine. Ford did not release the V-8 for commercial use until May 1932, and because of their intended use as

Ford's 1932 closed-cab Pickup resembled a Model A with its visor over the windshield. It was built on a production 1932 chassis with standard passenger car fenders, running boards, and hood. Here owner Paul King takes his mildly hot rodded version for a spin.

FORD'S 1932 SEDANS AND COMMERCIAL VEHICLES

working machines, most commercial pickup buyers preferred the reliable four-cylinder engine.

Ford's closed-cab pickup for 1932 resembled the Model A pickup with its boxy cab, short cowl, and visor over the windshield. Even the exterior door handles resembled, and were most likely, Model A components. The chassis components were all from the '32, including the fenders, hood, and headlight bar. Ford used a unique grille shell on the commercial vehicles. It resembled the one used on its passenger cars except the vertical bars were stamped as part of the shell and these bars were painted

Ford's open cab (Roadster) pickup became available in May 1932. Its soft top could not be folded, but it could be completely removed. The black top material was the same as that used on the Standard model Roadsters and Phaetons.

The bed on Ford's 1932 closed cab Pickup was painted the same color as the body. If pinstriping were ordered, it was only applied to the body and hood.

153 ■ DEUCE: 75 YEARS OF THE '32 FORD

CHAPTER SIX

Because of the lengthy pickup bed, all of Ford's 1932 pickup trucks were fitted with a side-mounted spare tire.

Ford's 1932 commercial models were fitted with a unique grille shell that had vertical stamped bars instead of a separate insert. The headlight bars on all commercial vehicles were black and did not have the center stainless piece.

black. The standard passenger car grille shell could still be ordered as an option. Ford painted the pickup's headlight bar black and did not have the stainless steel wrap on the span between the headlights or the chrome wire loom. Ford also painted the headlight buckets black.

Ford designed the interior of its pickups to be inexpensive and durable. They covered the seats on both the open and closed models with Black/Brown artificial leather. The door panels on the open pickup were trimmed with plain black Masonite panels and Ford covered the floor on both models with Ford's standard tan rubber mat. The windshield frame, instrument panel and other metal interior components were painted body color. The top and side curtains on the open pickup were made of a black rubberized fabric material. This top did not fold, but could be unbolted and removed as an entire assembly.

Because of the length of the bed, Ford located the gas tank under the seat on both models. This extra length also meant that there would be no rear bumper or rear-mounted spare. If a spare tire was ordered, it had to be a side mount. Ford offered the same color selection for the pickups as its passenger car lineup with a few additions.

Ford's 1932 pickup trucks used remaining Model A hardware such as this exterior door handle.

154 ■ DEUCE: 75 YEARS OF THE '32 FORD

Initially there were no complimentary colors for the belt molding. After May 1932, Ford gave its pickup customers the option of having the body's belt moldings painted for an extra cost. Pinstriping could also be selected for an additional charge. The pickup beds were painted body color, but never striped.

1932 Ford Panel Truck

In addition to a Sedan Delivery based on the passenger car, Ford also produced a larger Panel Delivery Model B-79. This model, first released in May 1932, offered a substantial storage area that measured 48-1/2 inches wide by 72-1/2 inches long. Unlike other 1932 all-metal

Ford's largest commercial vehicle created on the passenger car platform was this panel truck. This particular 1932 panel truck is owned by Paul Gommi. It was originally Washington Blue and was owned by an appliance repairman. Prior to selling it decades ago he painted it green. Gommi has cleaned off enough of the green paint to allow the original lettering to show through.

The vertical grille bars in the grille shell on Ford's 1932 commercial vehicles were painted black. Ford painted the windshield frame on the roadster pickup body color. (Photo Courtesy David Newhardt)

155 ■ DEUCE: 75 YEARS OF THE '32 FORD

bodies, Ford constructed its Panel Delivery with an internal framework of wood, wrapping sheet metal on the outside. Engineers constructed the floor of the cargo area using hard maple and added metal skid strips. The sides of the cargo area were covered with Masonite. This body, while similar to the 1933, was unique to 1932.

Hot Rod 1932 Ford Sedans and Commercial Vehicles

The last of the 1932 Fords to be accepted into the hot rod fold were the sedans and commercial vehicles. They had always been seen as family cars or work vehicles. While sedans were the most plentiful of the 1932 Ford models, they lacked the style of a Coupe or Roadster. But in the 1950s, hot rodders started to see the value in any 1932 Ford and began to build hot rods based on the sedan and commercial bodies. The first were the two-door sedans. Most of these cars needed very little bodywork and were brought back to life because of their low cost. Modifications to the body usually included chopping the top. It made a statement that this family car was now a hot rod.

In the late 1950s, two Detroit friends, Gordie Craig and Jim Seleski, were among the first to build a hot rod show car out of a 1932 Ford two-door sedan. It all started in 1958 with an ad in the local paper for a $90 '32 Ford two-door sedan—it was just the body on a frame. They wanted to build a hot rod, but they also wanted a

This is how a new 1932 Ford panel truck would have been delivered to the dealer—with the side mounted wheel in place but without a tire. Panel trucks were equipped with a single light on the left rear door. Unlike most other 1932 Ford models, this body has a lot of wood structure behind the exterior sheet metal panels.

Customers could order a Deluxe version of any of Ford's 1932 commercial vehicles including the panel truck. When ordered, a standard passenger car grille shell was included. The cowl lights and special paint scheme were not available from the factory.

When friends Gordie Craig and Jim Seleski searched the local Detroit newspaper in 1958, this is what they found advertised for $90. In the true spirit of hot rodding, they pooled their money and talents to turn this forlorn Model B into a show car.

FORD'S 1932 SEDANS AND COMMERCIAL VEHICLES

With metal finishing skills learned by trial and error, Craig and Seleski were able to repair their sedan's body and channel it over the frame. They channeled it because they wanted it low, but didn't feel they had the skills to chop the top. This photo was taken at Detroit's Autorama in 1962.

Like most hot rods built in that era, Craig and Seleski chose a flathead engine. The new overhead valve engines were available, but flatheads were less expensive. The exhaust system on the sedan was porcelain plated.

car in which they could double date. A Coupe or Roadster with a rumble seat was out of the question. The sedan would be perfect.

Like most Midwestern hot rodders, they learned about hot rods by reading *Hot Rod* magazine. There they saw how the California builders created their hot rods. But the East Coast and Midwest each had its own particular hot rod style that was different than that found in California. The wealth of closed cars originally sold in the Midwest and East Coast meant that more coupes and sedans would be turned into hot rods. The sedan Craig and Seleski found needed some body

157 ■ DEUCE: 75 YEARS OF THE '32 FORD

CHAPTER SIX

Gordie Craig (sitting on front tire) eventually bought out partner Jim Seleski's portion of the sedan. Craig painted this sedan in a one-car garage with a homemade spray setup. The color is Dodge truck red.

repair. They wanted it low, but didn't have the skills to chop a top. However, they figured out how to channel it.

Although highboys were the pattern for California hot rods, channeled cars were the style for the Midwest and East Coast. This penchant for channeling may have been a direct result of cars that had been ravaged by the extremes of weather and in need of floor pans and lower body rust repair.

With the car well underway, Craig and Seleski went to the DMV office to get the title. It was there that they found out that they had bought a *stolen car*. They were put in touch with the legal owner who at first wanted the sedan back. He relented and told Craig and Seleski that they could have the car's title, along with the hood, fenders, seats, and the rest of the parts from the car for $90. Craig and Seleski agreed and quickly sold off the parts for more than the $90 it cost them.

What started out as a simple street rod in which to double date slowly evolved into a show car. All of the chassis and engine components that could be chrome

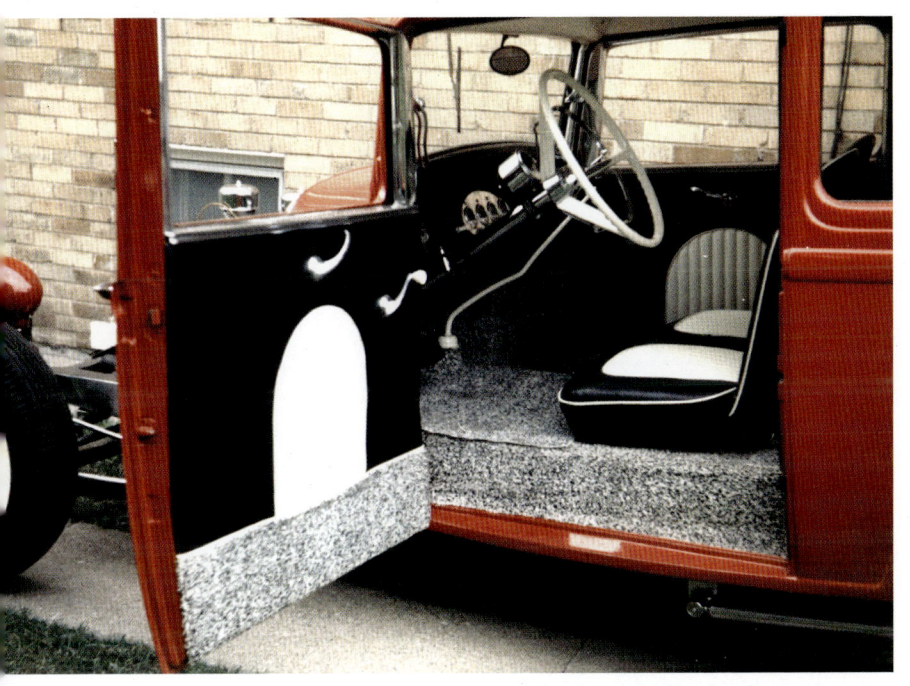

In 1959, there was only one catalog from which to buy hot rod parts—J.C. Whitney—and that's where the headliner came from. The seats are out of a Crosley and the carpeting came from K-Mart.

plated were plated. In the late 1950s, Detroit hot rodders in need of chrome plating made the short trip across the Ambassador Bridge to a small chrome shop in Windsor, Ontario, Canada. Craig and Seleski made this trip several times. In January of 1960, the car made its first showing (in primer) in Detroit and it took a trophy in the Unfinished class. That summer a lot of work was put into the sedan to have it completed for the car show held concurrently with the NHRA U.S. Nationals. That summer, Craig bought out Seleski for full ownership.

Craig was an ordinary hard-working guy who made extra money painting cars for friends. He jury-rigged a spray setup created from an old refrigeration compressor. His spray booth was a small, one-car garage in Detroit. "I used to buy surplus lacquer for $1 a gallon from Acme Automobile Paint Supply," says Craig. "I'd shoot on 20 coats and buff off 10 for a decent finish." He painted the sedan himself and the paint he used for the sedan (Dodge truck red) came directly from the Detroit Ditzler plant. "I had a friend who worked at Ditzler. He brought out a pint of paint a day hidden in his lunch box."

Like so many cars of the era, Craig's sedan featured a full-house flathead. One of the unique features of the car was its porcelain-plated exhaust system. "I took the entire exhaust system to Detroit Stove and had it white porcelain-plated," says Craig. Unfortunately, most people thought the headers and pipes were just painted gloss white. Craig trimmed the interior in black and white. He used Crosley bucket seats in the front. A chrome gas tank was placed on the floor in the rear. The headliner was ordered out of a J.C. Whitney catalog and the salt-and-pepper carpeting came from K-Mart.

Between 1960 and 1964, Craig took his sedan to 15 major car shows, garnering 22 awards. And like most Midwestern hot rods, it was never featured in a magazine. In 1965, Craig sold his red sedan for $1,500. Like most 1932 Fords, its component parts have been widely spread with certain parts showing up on other cars. The body is rumored to be in Texas.

Hot Rod Four-Door Sedans

The last of the 1932 Fords to be seriously stylized by hot rod enthusiasts are the four-door sedans. These family cars have always been shunned because of their stogy looks and two extra doors. While Ford built over 27,000 1932 four-door sedans, many were used up in the 1940s and 1950s as jalopy racers. Others were dismantled as parts cars for various coupe and roadster projects. Two modern-day owners, Jon Hall and Chuck de Heras, have looked at this once forgotten model in a new light. What they have done to their four-door sedans has opened the eyes of many hot rodders to a wide range of possibilities. The important thing is to create an individual hot rod that is fun to drive, especially if you can take several friends along for the ride.

Chuck de Heras picked the best local Southern California talent to build his four-door sedan. He went to hot rod fabricator Pete Eastwood to assemble the traditionally buggy sprung chassis using American Stamping rails. The Kennedy Brothers of Pomona did the 3-1/2 inch chop and Bob Bauder coordinated the build. All are highly talented and well-respected hot rod builders.

The engine de Heras selected came out of a 1960 Corvette. A friend of his who builds cars called him one day and wanted to know if he wanted a complete 1960 Corvette fuel-injected engine and four-speed transmission. Apparently, a customer brought in a 1960 Corvette and wanted to pull the original engine and transmission and replace it with a "better running" crate 350 and an

CHAPTER SIX

To stand out in today's hot rod world, Chuck de Heras built a chopped four-door sedan. The four-door was the last of the '32 body styles to be developed into a hot rod.

automatic transmission. de Heras gladly bought the number matching assembly for his sedan. The engine provided de Heras with another component for the car— the accent color for the wheels and pinstriping. The Chevrolet engine orange wheels and pinstriping blended well with the shade of brown selected that is similar to the original Ford Dark Winterleaf Brown.

For the interior, de Heras selected a material that had been used in Ford trucks in the 1970s. It resembles the original mohair Ford used in 1932. To round out

FORD'S 1932 SEDANS AND COMMERCIAL VEHICLES

The engine in de Heras' sedan is straight out of a 1960 Corvette, complete with the fuel injection unit, chrome ignition shielding, and four-speed transmission. The engine's color, Chevrolet Engine Orange, was the inspiration for the color of the wheels and pinstriping.

this unique retro look, the instrument panel and window frames received a wood grain finish similar to what would have been added when this car was new.

Chuck de Heras' 1932 Ford four-door looks like a vintage hot rod because of its black frame, factory-style paint scheme, and mohair interior. Its small-block Chevy engine didn't come out of a wooden crate and it has a rare Rochester fuel-injection unit on top. The shifter sticking out of the floor really shifts the gears.

The interior of de Heras' sedan is upholstered in a material very similar to the original Rose Beige mohair. He's even incorporated a wood grain finish on the instrument panel and window frames similar to that in the original Deluxe models.

161 ■ DEUCE: 75 YEARS OF THE '32 FORD

Scale Model '32 Fords

There probably isn't a hot rodder alive who hasn't built a model car from a kit at least once in their life. AMT's 3-in-1 '32 Ford kit is one that should lead the list. West Gallogy, Sr., a Detroit attorney, founded AMT in 1948. Gallogy's first car was a die-cast aluminum Ford sedan that was available only through Ford dealers. Gallogy developed a relationship with Ford to become its primary supplier of promotional model cars. To meet the need, Gallogy opened Aluminum Model Toys in Detroit. By the late 1940s, the outdated method of using die-cast aluminum to make the bodies for model cars was replaced by injection molding of plastic. In addition to being cheaper to produce, plastic could also be molded in colors. This eliminated the extra step of painting. Gallogy quickly changed the name of his company to AMT and invested in injection molding machines.

In the early 1950s, Gallogy hired George Toteff, an experienced pattern maker, to run the company. Toteff changed the way the company did business by farming out the injection molding to the best local firms, while keeping design in-house. In 1958, AMT took a gamble with the idea of taking the promotional models it was making for the auto industry and offering them to retail outlets as unassembled kits. AMT added fender skirts, flames, and lake pipes and created the 3-in-1 (stock, custom, or race) model kit. In 1959, AMT released its first antique car kit—a Model B 1932 Ford Roadster for $1.25. Now all the kids who were too young to own a real hot rod could build the Deuce of their dreams. While the kit offered an optional small-block Chevy engine, a pair of chrome wheels and slicks, the young hot rodders who had been reading *Rod & Custom* or *Hot Rod* knew that the guys who were building real hot rods cannibalized other cars for engines and parts. Soon, there would be a new Pontiac kit sitting on the shelf minus the engine and a new Chevrolet kit minus the steering wheel and wheels—donor cars for a miniature hot rod. Almost anything a real hot rodder did with an actual '32 Ford Roadster could be reproduced in 1/25 scale on a 10-year-old kid's basement workbench. As kids, we chopped, channeled, and lowered our little model cars. We shaved the grille shell and adjusted the stance. It was hot rod heaven on a small scale.

AMT followed the success of its '32 Roadster with the V-8 powered 3-in-1 five-window coupe. By the early 1960s, AMT was producing almost every modern American car in 1/25 scale kit form. Young men who loved hot rods soon saw the release of AMT's 1940 Ford sedan and coupe. Every beloved real hot rod was now available in polystyrene plastic. I've built dozens.

AMT was not alone in the model car market. John Hanley started his scale model business in 1947. In 1955 he received contracts from Chrysler and GM to produce promotional models and he quickly formed his company, Jo-Han. In 1959, Jo-Han also released 3-in-1 scale model kits. In 1963, George Toteff left AMT to form MPC. In the early- and mid-1960s, each of these companies hired big name custom car builders like Barris, Cushenberry, Winfield, and Jeffries to style their model cars.

By the 1970s, the kids who had built model cars in the 1960s now had their own real cars, along with a few kids of their own. The fascination with cars, real or model, waned as high gas prices and insurance premiums took away the incentive to invest, financially or emotionally, in something that consumers found no longer interesting.

The model car industry was also undergoing changes. In 1977, Lesney, the company that created Matchbox models, bought AMT and moved it to Baltimore, Maryland. In the early 1980s they sold AMT to ERTL. General Mills bought MPC and then sold it to ERTL, who folded its model line into AMT/ERTL. Jo-Han continued to release models using its original tooling until 1991, when it was bought by Seville, an OEM plastics manufacturer. Seville soon lost interest and the Jo-Han models passed into history.

The 1990s saw a renewed interest in model cars. This was primarily driven by NASCAR racing and by the interest the collectible die-cast models its teams were selling. Those once youthful model builders, who were no longer interested in building model cars, could buy a die-cast model ready to place on the shelf. The NASCAR die-cast models set a trend for the production of other die-cast models, including hot rods. The yellow '32 Ford coupe from the movie *American Graffiti* was one of the first to be reproduced. This interest in model cars encouraged one of the original manufacturers to get back in the business—AMT/ERTL started making 1/25 scale plastic kits of the *American Graffiti* coupe. Many of the older 1932 Ford kits were also re-released.

Today's modern model car kits are much more detailed than anything produced in the early 1960s. They take more time and skill to assemble than the kits I built as a ten-year-old in my parents' Michigan basement.

FORD'S 1932 SEDANS AND COMMERCIAL VEHICLES

John Hall's Four-Door Hot Rod

Jon Hall is a long-time Michigan-based hot rodder. In his life, he has built a variety of cars; but this time he took a slightly different approach. His initial concept was to build an exceptionally low '32 Ford. He never intended to build a four-door, but fate intervened and his vision became clear. What he saw was a fun hot rod into which he could pile several of his friends for a drive to lunch. In doing so he created a hot rod with maximum interior space and comfort while not compromising on an aggressive hot rod stance.

Hall owns several '32 Ford hot rods and they all have something about them that is unusual and innovative. With this Deuce his only intention was to have a car that sat exceptionally low, had excellent road manners, and offered a superior ride. He never intended to build a four-door, but he found an ad in *Hemmings Motor News* for a four-door body in Texas. The owner wanted to take his complete original four-door sedan and replace the body with a Brookville roadster. "This was a perfect rust-free body complete with the interior," says Hall. He bought it for $5,500.

Hall wanted to make his four-door as comfortable inside as possible. He dropped the floors in both the front and the rear to create more legroom. He also moved the front kick panels out as far as possible. Then he raised the rear seat by four inches for "stadium-style" seating. Glide manufactured the front seat, which is adjustable fore and aft. This facilitates entry into the rear seat. Then everything was wrapped in red leather.

By raising rear seat, a deep 4-inch "C" notch could be put in the rear of the frame allowing the car to sit as low as possible over the rear axle. Because the car's stance is so low, Hall raised the rear wheel openings up 3-3/4 inches. Because of the weight differential with people in or out of

Michigan based hot rod builder Jon Hall took a slightly different approach to making his four-door sedan stand out. He wanted the car as low as possible without chopping the top. He used an air suspension in the rear and raised the rear wheel openings 3 3/4 inches. Here, Hall is behind the wheel with engine builder Mark Kirby in the passenger seat.

163 ■ DEUCE: 75 YEARS OF THE '32 FORD

CHAPTER SIX

The rear seat in Hall's four-door has been raised by 4 inches. This provides plenty of room for a six-footer while providing space under the seat for the air compressor that controls the height of the rear suspension. Hall has retained the original window regulators, armrests, and ashtrays.

the back seat, a regular rear spring couldn't maintain the car's stance. So, Hall added an air ride suspension to the rear. This allows him to preserve the car's low stance with a back seat full of football players or when riding solo. The dropped floor pans required some creative exhaust work to keep all of the pipes above the frame line. Hall added heat shields around the mufflers to prevent heat from entering the passenger compartment.

Hall stepped up and added the holy grail of flatheads—an Ardun built by flathead expert Mark Kirby.

Hall loves to drive his hot rods and often loads up several friends for a trip to a local diner. The inviting interior is covered in red leather. The floor has been dropped for extra legroom.

164 ■ DEUCE: 75 YEARS OF THE '32 FORD

FORD'S 1932 SEDANS AND COMMERCIAL VEHICLES

What do you do when you only have a few pieces from a rusted out '32 sedan? If you're Elwood Peterson, you nail them to the wall of your barn. The foreshortened look is because of the addition of a door from a five-window coupe. Also hidden in the rafters of his barn is a complete '32 five-window.

John Couch's '32 sedan was built in the 1970s with road handling in mind. The wheels are 1970s-vintage basket weave with 60 series radial tires.

165 ■ DEUCE: 75 YEARS OF THE '32 FORD

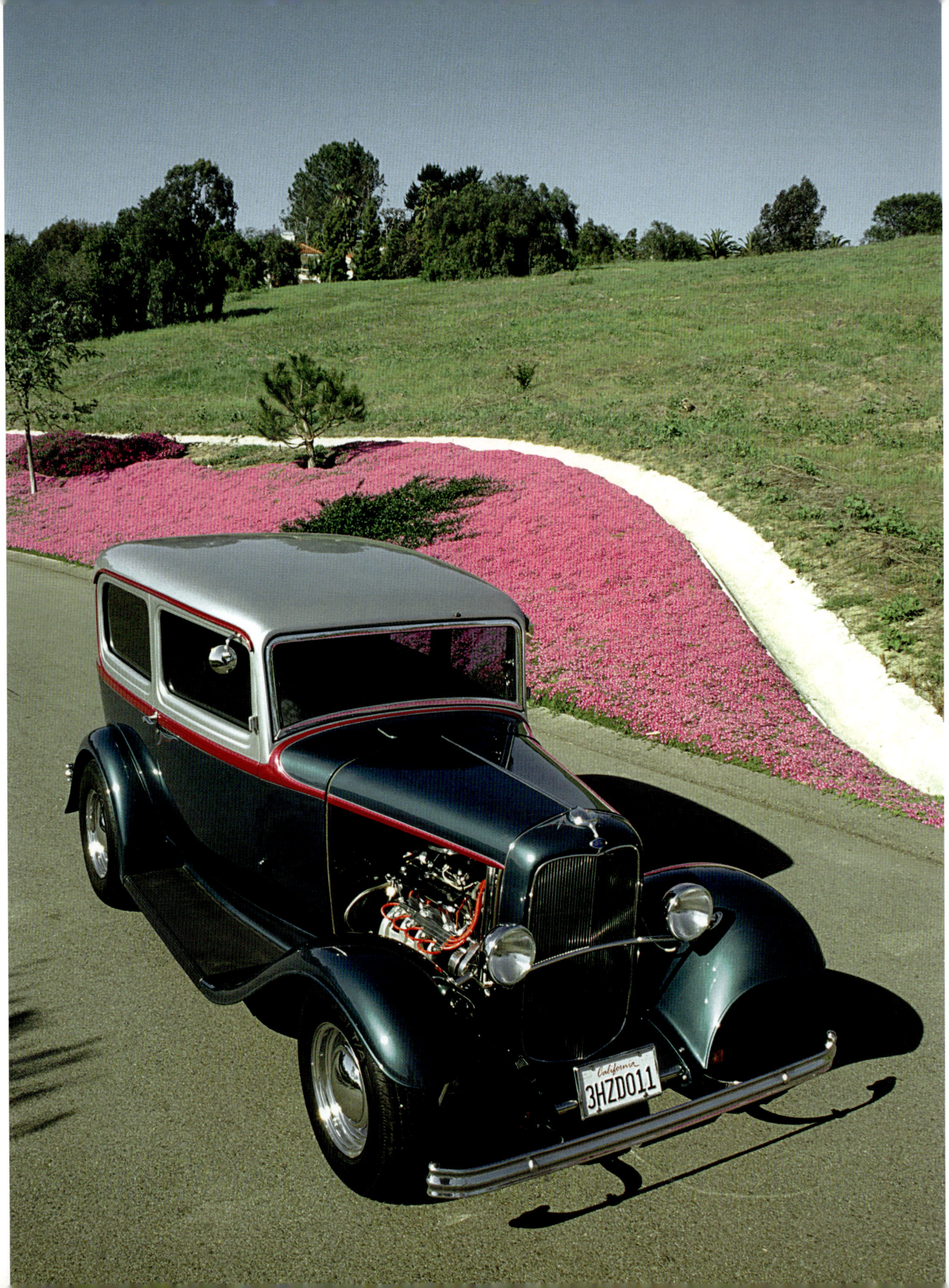
California
3HZD011

FORD'S 1932 SEDANS AND COMMERCIAL VEHICLES

The profile of Don Carpenter's '32 Victoria clearly defines the continental styling look Ford wanted to create with this model. The nose-down stance of this full-fendered sedan is also executed perfectly. The tires have the correct stagger and are positioned perfectly within the wheel openings. It's an excellent blending of all the wonderful attributes of the original '32 Ford with the hot rod influence.

The engine has been bored and stroked to displace 292 cubic inches. It has forged pistons, water-cooled main bearings, a full flow oil filter, and a Howard cam. On top are four Stromberg two-barrel carburetors. Inside the chrome generator housing is an alternator. The transmission is a T-5 five-speed driving through a 9-inch Ford rear end.

These two owners have proven that what may at one time have been the most undesirable of 1932 Ford

Left: *In addition to the vivid color combination, this '32 sedan has had its roof filled. This was accomplished by finding a late-model station wagon roof that has the correct crown (in both directions) for the plug. It then took careful welding and metal finishing to make it appear as though it came from the factory this way.*

What better way to tow a sprint car than with a chopped '32 Ford sedan? This must have been an impressive sight in 1952 when this photo was taken.

CHAPTER SIX

Henry Astor is the executive director of the American Hot Rod Foundation and the owner of this highboy sedan. The thousands of historical hot rod images he's seen must have influenced the look of his sedan.

When Astor bought his sedan the top had already been chopped and filled. To keep the nostalgic feel of a vintage hot rod, builder Dave Crouse created a vinyl-covered panel that was bolted to the roof to resemble the original cloth insert.

168 ■ DEUCE: 75 YEARS OF THE '32 FORD

FORD'S 1932 SEDANS AND COMMERCIAL VEHICLES

Michigan-based hot rodder Kerry Pankow traded a '32 coupe for this sedan to be able to carry his kids along in comfort. He did the painting himself including the flames that blend from white, to yellow, to blue. The white wire wheels and wide whites work well with the flames.

A year before this photo of Pankow's sedan was shot, he was driving it without the fenders. Being able to easily add or remove the fenders makes the 1932 Ford one of the most versatile cars to hot rod.

bodies can be built into an attractive and highly functional hot rod. Imagine one of these sedans at the end of a line of roadsters. It would be the one you'd go to first. Look for more 1932 Ford four-door hot rods in the future.

Ford's 1932 sedans and commercial vehicles were the last to join the hot rod party. But in a hot rod world dominated by roadsters and coupes, they have proven to be the most interesting and a virtual blank canvas for inventive builders. All of the traditional hot rod tricks work well on these models and the results are often striking. As the desire to build hot rods from original '32s continues, more and more builders will look to these once-orphaned models to create memorable hot rods.

DEUCE: 75 YEARS OF THE '32 FORD

CHAPTER SEVEN

The Future of the 1932 Ford

Jack Kuttner's '32 three-window coupe is built with a fiberglass body. Today's fiberglass reproduction bodies have all the correct proportions of the original Ford bodies and are reasonably priced.

THE FUTURE OF THE 1932 FORD

In 2007, the 1932 Ford celebrates its 75th anniversary as the world's most popular hot rod. One would tend to think there might be a new contender to displace the 1932 Ford from its place in the hot rodding world, but it's not going to happen. The 1932 Ford is as popular as ever and will most likely be more popular when it hits its 100th anniversary in 2032.

The mystique of the 1932 Ford has been bottled and sold by the many manufacturers of reproduction fiberglass and steel bodies. It would be natural to conclude that once knock-offs are made for half the price of an original, the market for originals would be devalued. Not so in the world of 1932 Fords. The addition of high-quality fiberglass and new steel bodies has increased the value and desirability of original steel bodies. Just as Elvis impersonators honor the memory and legend of one of rock and roll's greatest personalities, the reproduction bodies honor the hot rod icon, the 1932 Ford.

Fiberglass reproduction bodies first surfaced in the 1960s. They were often crudely built with poor proportions and poor workmanship. At the time these bodies were not intended to be perfect copies, but simply to represent the shape of a 1932 Ford for racing cars. These bodies were lighter and less expensive than an original steel body. Spectators sitting in the stands could not tell they were fiberglass and the racers didn't have to worry about minor damage. As hot rodding evolved, so did the market for the fiberglass body. In the 1970s, high-quality reproductions were available. Companies like Gibbon

Bob Berry's chopped three-window coupe body came from the molds at Wescott. Finding and chopping an original three-window body is an expensive proposition. A fiberglass reproduction body saves the builder in many ways.

CHAPTER SEVEN

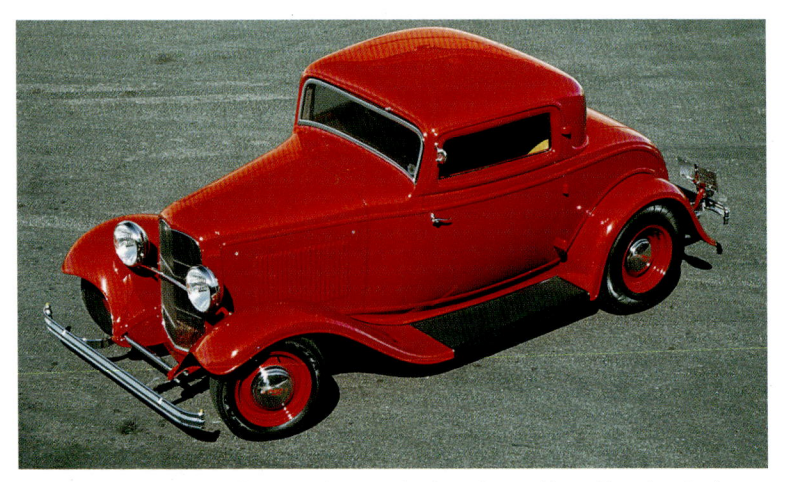

Phil Brooks' three-window was built with a Gibbon fiberglass body. Its working cowl vent, exposed door hinges, and chrome windshield frame camouflage the fact that this is a reproduction body.

and Westcott were building roadster bodies that looked exactly like the originals and could be easily repaired. Soon hot rodders were buying these improved bodies and building righteous hot rods with them.

Dee Wescott is considered a pioneer in the art of making fiberglass reproduction 1932 Fords. His first 1932 Ford Roadster body, built in 1974, is still on the road today. Wescott opened Wescott's Auto Restyling in 1954. It was a combination body shop and hot rod shop located in Damascus, Oregon. He learned the art of working with fiberglass when damaged Corvettes were brought to him for repair. It was in late 1954 that he made his first reproduction part out of fiberglass. It was a rear splash pan for a 1934 Ford. His fiberglass business quickly expanded when he began making fiberglass gas tank covers for a boat company. In the late 1950s, Wescott started to make fenders and other reproduction parts for hot rods.

In the 1970s, Wescott started to build complete cars. He started with Model As and a '32 Roadster. These cars were given VIN numbers and licensed as new vehicles. The ever-increasing government requirements and liability issues forced Wescott to abandon the idea of making complete cars, but the parts business continued and expanded. So did the reproduction body business.

Wescott used a different approach to building his reproduction bodies. While others were using wood as the structure of their fiberglass bodies, Wescott installed a full steel cage, much like the support structure used on

Don Prieto's '32 Roadster is fitted with a fiberglass body built by Harwood Industries. When Harwood built their molds, they increased the length of the door by two inches.

THE FUTURE OF THE 1932 FORD

the early Corvettes he repaired. Wescott went a step further by installing a side door guard beam, similar to the ones installed in all the new cars for passenger side impact protection. On his '32 coupe body he also installed shoulder harness mounts. Today, Wescott manufactures two 1932 three-window bodies: one with a stock height roof and one with a 2-1/2 inch chop. He also builds a '32 Roadster and a '32 Phaeton. The roadster and three-window can be configured with either a trunk or a rumble seat. A full line of options for each body includes stock or hidden hinges, working cowl vent, and power windows.

Fiberglass 1932 Ford bodies have been manufactured for over 30 years, making hot rodding available to the masses. Initially, the popularity of the 1932 Ford Roadster drove this industry, but soon other body styles were being produced. In addition to reproduction bodies, enthusiasts can purchase reproduction '32 frame rails and complete chassis assemblies. This allows a wider audience for hot rodding and the 1932 Ford.

Brookville Roadster and Coupe

Brookville Roadster Company in southwestern Ohio is where Ray Gollahon started making a few Model A patch panels in 1971. When he took his parts to the Hershey swap meet in 1972, they quickly sold out. What started out as a side job of making a few body panels has now grown into a business dedicated to making complete car bodies.

Brookville Roadster Company is the leading supplier of steel 1932 Ford Roadster bodies. Here, the finishing touches are being put on several freshly assembled bodies.

CHAPTER SEVEN

Brookville reverse-engineered an original '32 Ford Roadster to make the dies for the one they produce. Here a body is being assembled using an original Model B cowl.

In addition to bodies, Brookville makes fenders for 1932 Fords. They even roll a wire into the outside edge, using machinery dating back to the 1930s.

In addition to being a hot rodder, Ray Gollahon is also a skilled sheet metal worker. He started making Model A patch panels because Ford produced more Model As than any other model. The success of these small components eventually grew into making entire Model A bodies. Today, Brookville manufactures both the '28–'29 and '30–'31 Ford Roadsters and roadster pickup models of each.

174 ■ DEUCE: 75 YEARS OF THE '32 FORD

THE FUTURE OF THE 1932 FORD

Brookville also makes '32 Ford grille shells. Stacked up on the floor are the blanks used to create the shell and off to the right is a stack after the first hit from the press.

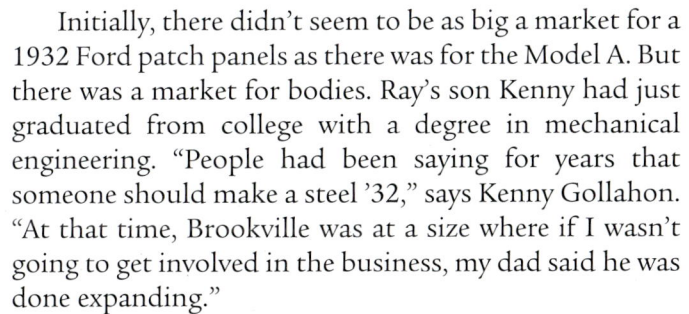

This is the die Brookville uses to stamp out its 1932 Ford grille shells. For durability, this die is made of hardened steel.

Initially, there didn't seem to be as big a market for a 1932 Ford patch panels as there was for the Model A. But there was a market for bodies. Ray's son Kenny had just graduated from college with a degree in mechanical engineering. "People had been saying for years that someone should make a steel '32," says Kenny Gollahon. "At that time, Brookville was at a size where if I wasn't going to get involved in the business, my dad said he was done expanding."

With the younger Gollahon on board, they started working on a complete '32 Ford Roadster body. They decided not to reinvent the wheel, but to use the original 1932 Ford Roadster as the prototype for their new body. "The biggest challenge we faced in making a '32 Ford body was replicating what Henry Ford had done," says Gollahon. They pulled plaster molds off the original body. Then they calculated the shrinkages and created the tooling. "Dad used to have a tool and die shop and he made all the Model A tooling out of hard steel," says Gollahon. "But all the new tooling is being made from Kirksite." Kirksite is used for short run dies. It's an alloy of aluminum and zinc that's malleable and can be welded. Kirksite dies are good for as many as 1,500 parts before any wear is noticed. It is possible to add a hardened steel insert to an area of high wear to extend the life of a Kirksite die indefinitely. "We're at about 600 '32

Roadster bodies produced so far and from the first one to now, we can't detect any wear on the dies," says Gollahon. A large run for Brookville is 2,000 parts. Eventually Brookville will build 2,000 '32 Roadster bodies, but at the pace of 150 a year, it will be 10 years before they reach that number.

The 1932 Ford Roadster body that Brookville manufactures is a direct replacement for the original. "We didn't make any changes to the '32 Roadster body," says Gollahon. "We didn't change any bracing or lengthen the doors. People want what Henry Ford produced. That's what carried this company to where it is now." The change that Brookville made was to leave out the little reveal on the quarter panel where the tank strip would dive into the quarter; instead, they made it smooth in that area. It was an area prone to cracking, so that one small change served to strengthen the quarter panel. They also offer a flat floor. In addition, they offer a deck former option that pinches off the inside where the package tray usually is. This gives the body a little more strength. They didn't change any of the bracing and all of the components interchange with those on an original 1932 Ford Roadster.

The success of their roadster encouraged Brookville to look toward building another 1932 Ford body—the three-window coupe. "The market is ready for a nice steel

175 ■ DEUCE: 75 YEARS OF THE '32 FORD

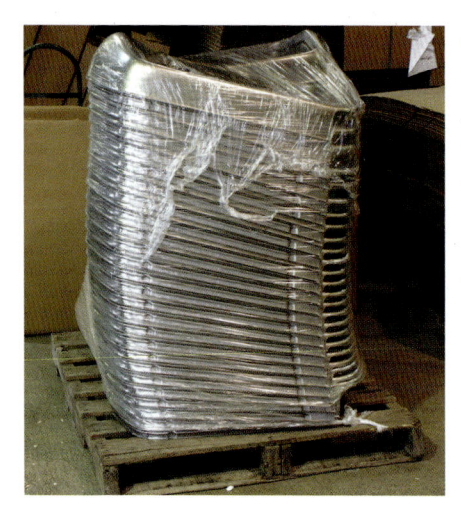

CHAPTER SEVEN

Here's a stack of Brookville '32 Ford grille shells that are ready to ship. Each year they manufacture 1,500 '32 Ford grille shells and 150 '32 Ford Roadster bodies.

Brookville realized that there is a high demand for a steel three-window coupe body, so they started to produce components and complete bodies. Just like the roadster, they reverse-engineered an original body. This is their first complete three-window body.

coupe," says Gollahon. "If you find an original coupe today, it's missing either the doors, deck lid, garnish moldings, or dash—and then they want $18,000 for that shell." Gollahon also listened to his customer base and realized that the three-window coupe was more popular than the five-window. It was a gamble that would cost Brookville over one million dollars to produce the first body.

Brookville started with a cherry three-window coupe that Gollahon Sr. has had since the early 1960s. Brookville approached the same company that did the tooling for the Roadster to do the three-window. The original three-window body was digitally scanned and a computer model was created. They found slight variances from side to side. "We didn't change any of that," says Gollahon. "The main reason we didn't is that if we make the right door just like the left door, then whenever we sell a right door, it might not fit the opening in an original stock body." While today's manufactured automobiles are an exact mirror image right to left, cars of the 1930s were only approximate matches. Brookville also had another complete three-window body used for fitting their reproduction components. They have been able to switch original parts to their body and reproduction parts to the original body without any problems. The biggest variance they have found in the original bodies is in how the lower edge of the deck lid was hemmed. "In 1932, Ford was simply building a car," says Gollahon. "It isn't like today where someone is spending $100,000 for a new car and wants the best fit possible."

The three-window body by Brookville is made exactly like Ford engineers made it in 1932, right down to the

Stashed all around Brookville's Ohio facility are original '32 Ford bodies. This three-window is one of the bodies used during the reverse engineering process to create the dies for their coupe.

176 ■ DEUCE: 75 YEARS OF THE '32 FORD

wooden inner structure. "When you look at this car, you think it's a preserved three-window body," says Gollahon. Brookville did make one change to the way the body is assembled. Brookville stamped the entire side as one piece, in the same way modern cars are done. This keeps the door openings consistent. Ford originally designed the three-window with several components making up the perimeter of the door opening. A slight shift during assembly could make a significant change in the door opening. "With that body side being one piece," says Gollahon. "It saves us from trying to assemble the window post." The roof on the new coupe will be open like the original. Since the body was modeled in the computer, they have the data to make a fill panel with the correct curvature.

All of the 1932 three-window coupes that Brookville produces will have a stock-height roof. "No chopped top," says Gollahon. "If we chop it 2 inches someone will want 2.5, if we chop it 3 inches they are going to want something else. We'll never win and we'd have to have an entirely new set of tooling dies for the doors moldings and body side." Brookville will have an approved list of fabricators around the country that will be able to do an excellent job of chopping the new coupe to any owner's specification. Also, by sticking to only building stock components, Brookville can service the parts market for the owner of an original three-window body who needs garnish moldings, a door, or a deck lid. "We make it identical to stock and that's been our staple," says Gollahon.

In addition to complete Model A and 1932 Ford Roadster and coupe bodies, Brookville also makes grille shells, running boards, aprons, and fenders. They also stamp out 1,500 '32 grille shells a year. This is a testament to the love of the '32 Ford and the adaptability of the '32 shell to other hot rod variants.

Brookville Roadster Company has been a godsend for hot rodders. The company has enhanced the entire hot rodding world with its exquisite steel bodies and components. The release of their three-window coupe will once again revolutionize the hot rodding world by providing an exact copy of Ford's three-window to those who have always dreamed of owning one.

Hot Rods and Horsepower Dearborn Deuce Convertible

The latest and one of the most interesting '32 Ford reproduction bodies to enter the hot rod world is the

The newest '32 Ford body being marketed by Hot Rods and Horsepower is their Dearborn Deuce convertible. It has the appearance of a Roadster, but it has roll-up windows like a Cabriolet.

CHAPTER SEVEN

This deck on the Dearborn Deuce convertible body opens, allowing the top to be completely hidden when down. They also stretched the door openings by two inches for added comfort.

Here's a Dearborn Deuce convertible body in bare steel ready for delivery. The rear deck is open and the top is partially folded.

Hot Rods and Horsepower Dearborn Deuce Convertible. Designers and engineers have combined the best of the original 1932 Ford Roadster and Cabriolet to develop a new body style that looks like a roadster, but has the weatherproof roll-up windows of a Cabriolet. Unlike the two original cars, the top on the Dearborn Deuce convertible is completely hidden when down. This new body is being built for Hot Rods and Horsepower by ASC (American Specialty Cars) of Detroit.

Hot Rods and Horsepower made several subtle changes to the original Ford Roadster to create this new package and preserve the original look. First, the doors were stretched by three inches. The original roadster's door openings are small and the additional length makes entry and exit much easier. The rear edge of the door also

178 ■ DEUCE: 75 YEARS OF THE '32 FORD

THE FUTURE OF THE 1932 FORD

The is the right hand inner cowl structure and hinge pillar of a Dearborn Deuce convertible body. A large rectangular section is welded in, giving the body extra strength and rigidity.

meets the leading edge of the top, creating a pleasing line. They also reshaped the front edge of the door to bring the glass forward. Finally, they reshaped the cowl to accept a unique windshield that meets the side glass. The new side glass is also curved and custom-made for this body.

Hot Rods and Horsepower created an opening behind the seat to store the entire top assembly. They also deepened the cockpit by carving out an additional 2.5 inches from this panel. This additional space is given back in passenger legroom. Even with all of these changes, the outer dimensions of the body remain stock. With the top up, these revisions give the car a trendy long nose, short deck look.

Hot Rods and Horsepower selected a top covered with high-quality Cambria cloth. To give a custom look to the interior, they also offer an optional full headliner. Their top features a glass rear window and comes in several attractive colors. Because the passenger compartment is completely closed, the car can be fully air conditioned or heated, making it an all-weather roadster.

To celebrate the 75th year of the Deuce, Hot Rods and Horsepower has partnered with GM, DaimlerChrysler, and of course Ford to create limited editions of their Dearborn Deuce convertible. Each manufacturer will create a hot rod based upon the unique convertible body. Each manufacturer will add signature engines, chassis, and styling touches. The goal is to celebrate the 75th anniversary of the '32 Ford with 100 of each special version. These special "Anniversary Deuces" will be delivered in 2006, so owners can enjoy them for the entire anniversary year of 2007.

Each corporate design team for these special hot rods will create a distinctive hood, grille shell, and grille insert. They will also create a custom interior with special instrumentation. Each will add an exclusive exterior

For the 75th anniversary of the 1932 Ford, Ford Motor Company will create a special Dearborn Deuce convertible. Ford's car will look traditional by featuring a stock grille shell and hood. Under the hood will be a 4.6-liter DOHC engine and an electronic fuel injection unit with individual chrome-plated stacks to mimic the look of a vintage Hilborn unit.

CHAPTER SEVEN

Carroll Shelby will be joining in the 75th anniversary celebration of the 1932 Ford with his own version of the Dearborn Deuce convertible. The look of his deuce has been inspired by his fabled Cobra.

color with a coordinated top color. Each company will use their model to showcase one of their popular and powerful engines.

Ford is on point with their version of the Dearborn Deuce—their heritage demands it. The car they are building will be very traditional in style. Why would Ford mess with what they created 75 years earlier? Heading Ford's design team is Larry Erickson, designer of the new Ford Mustang. He's supported by Mark Robinson and Jamie Allison of Ford Racing, who will direct the construction of the special 4.6-liter Ford engine.

Because of Ford's design heritage, their car will have the most traditional look of the three, featuring a stock grille shell and hood. The underside will feature a Kugel independent rear end and Indy I-beam front suspension. The Ford team selected a 4.6-liter DOHC engine as a starting point. It will be internally upgraded and be finished with an electronic fuel injection unit that will look like a vintage Hilborn unit with individual chrome-plated stacks. There will also be a supercharged version as well as one with a single four-barrel carburetor. Backing this powerful combination will be a Tremec six-speed transmission or a Ford AOD automatic.

A Ford performance connection that goes back decades is being re-kindled with the celebration of the 75th anniversary of the 1932 Ford. Carroll Shelby has agreed to pay tribute to the 1932 Ford by creating 100 special Shelby Cobra Deuces. This special edition will have a powertrain similar to the one on the Ford model. The biggest difference will be in the Shelby Cobra styling cues and Shelby Blue paint. The wheels will be similar in design to those used on the original 427 Cobras. Instead of side pipes, the exhaust will emerge from the side of the frame, just in front of the rear wheel. A Cobra-style hood scoop and single chrome driver's roll bar will complete the look.

It's no surprise that Ford is celebrating the 75th anniversary of the 1932 Ford, but the addition of General Motors and DaimlerChrysler makes an unusually big

THE FUTURE OF THE 1932 FORD

The Dearborn Deuce convertible that DaimlerChrysler is going to build will have some art deco themes included with a retro Mopar look. One of the company's new Hemi engines will be under the hood.

statement. It would be hard to imagine the history of hot rodding without either one of these manufacturers. While Ford's 1932 models have become an outstanding platform for the hot rod, Chrysler and GM have contributed engines for thousands of memorable hot rods. The 350 Chevy engine is probably the most popular engine in hot rodding today and the Chrysler Hemi is legendary for the amount of power it could produce and for its distinctive looks. It is significant that both of these companies have stepped up to celebrate the greatest car in American hot rodding history—the 1932 Ford.

DaimlerChrysler's contribution to the 75th anniversary of the 1932 Ford will be a Dearborn Deuce convertible designed under the direction of Ralph Gilles. Gilles and his staff were responsible for the successful Chrysler 300. Their concept uses some of the art deco themes that inspired the 300's design. Their triangular grille is also reminiscent of Chrysler vehicles designed in the 1930s.

Powering the Chrysler Deuce will be one of their new Hemi engines. This engine, offered in the 300, Magnum, and Charger, quickly proved it had the performance chops to be listed in the same class as Chrysler's legendary original Hemi engines. Chrysler's goal is to pump up the horsepower to over 500. The Chrysler Deuce will borrow heavily from Chrysler's other performance cars for the creation of this one-of-a-kind hot rod.

General Motors has also given their RSVP to the Deuce's 75th anniversary party by signing up to build the Bow Tie Deuce. GM wants to create the best-handling '32 Ford by wrapping the Dearborn Deuce convertible body around a new Corvette chassis and engine. GM's Bow Tie Deuce will have a four-wheel independent suspension with a rear suspension built

Chevrolet's design team is approaching their version of the Dearborn Deuce just as seriously as any production car by creating a full-size clay model. Here the stylists sculpt the clay on the hood's side panel.

DEUCE: 75 YEARS OF THE '32 FORD

CHAPTER SEVEN

Chevrolet's design team will be creating their version of the Dearborn Deuce convertible called the Bow Tie Deuce. Of the three manufacturers, Chevrolet's Deuce will have the most sophisticated suspension.

THE FUTURE OF THE 1932 FORD

Bowtie Deuce 75th anniv.
side view studies

a

b

c

d

Chevrolet's stylists try many different combinations of hood sculpting details and wheel designs on paper long before production. Many never make it past this point.

This is Chevrolet's final design rendering of their version of the Dearborn Deuce convertible. Minor changes may be made prior to the first build.

from the best elements from the Cadillac CTS-V and Z06 Corvette. Two engine and transmission combinations will be available: (1) the 500-horsepower LS7, 427 cubic inch engine backed by a six-speed manual transmission or (2) a supercharged version of the Corvette LS2 backed by an automatic transmission. In stock form, the 364 cubic inch LS2 engine develops 400 horsepower.

GM's Bow Tie Deuce designers have borrowed from the designs of the early 1930s GM cars. The designers have leaned the 1934 Chevrolet grille back and added three large rectangular louvers to the sides of the hood. The interior will feature a steering wheel and center instrument cluster inspired by a classic 1950s Corvette.

Each of these cars will be extremely original in design, but with visual cues taken from its corporate parents and the original 1932 Ford. Each model will feature the latest in engines and drivelines and offer the buyer air conditioning and heat along with many other special amenities. In addition to Ford, both DaimlerChrysler and General Motors will be scheduling events to celebrate the 75th anniversary of the 1932 Ford and their involvement with this program.

183 ■ DEUCE: 75 YEARS OF THE '32 FORD

The Speedway Deuce Roadster

Bill Smith's Speedway Motors has made a dream come true for hot rodders. His Speedway Motors has been on the leading edge in kit hot rods and components for years. Now anyone can call Speedway's phone line or go to the Speedway website and order a complete 1932 Ford Roadster, minus the engine and transmission. Getting into hot rodding with an icon of the hot rodding world could not be any easier.

The Speedway Signature Series '32 Deuce Roadster comes in only one flavor—traditional red highboy. It features an all-steel body with a boxed frame and full chrome running gear. Speedway didn't cut corners on the interior. The bench seat is covered in leather and the carpets are wool. They have installed a 1940 Ford style instrument panel with full Stewart Warner instrumentation. Even the trunk is fully carpeted. Each car is fitted with a set of big-and-little BF Goodrich wide whitewall tires on steel wheels.

Bill Smith's Speedway Motors have been supplying hot rodders and racers with parts since 1952. Now Bill has stepped up to offer the ultimate hot rod component—an entire all-steel '32 Ford Roadster. All the buyer needs to do is install an engine.

THE FUTURE OF THE 1932 FORD

Speedway Motors' '32 Roadster has an instrument panel styled after the classic look of a 1940 Ford. It comes complete with gauges and a banjo-style steering wheel.

Speedway's Deuce includes a chrome dropped front axle and a 9-inch Ford rear axle. Even BFG wide white sidewall tires and wheels are included.

As of this writing, Speedway is planning to deliver four cars a month and the cost is just under $50,000. The only possible downside to what Speedway is producing is the fact that all of the roadsters will be identical. But a little creative wheel and tire swapping or the addition of a few flames and well-placed pinstriping will quickly personalize this slick roadster.

This isn't the first Deuce package that Speedway has offered. They also have a '32 lowboy roadster that they have marketed for years. It features a fiberglass body with 2-inch stretched door openings and a rolled rear pan. They recessed the firewall and built a transmission tunnel into the floor pan. It rides on a custom-built tubular chassis that lets the body sit low, giving the appearance of an original '32 Roadster that's been channeled. It has the looks and attitude of a channeled '32 Roadster, but at a much lower cost.

CHAPTER SEVEN

Highly Styled Deuces

In addition to building Deuces with tradition in mind, many builders have taken a different path that includes completely restyling the '32 Ford body while retaining all the original styling cues. The most notable of these are the Boydsters, built by Boyd Coddington. Coddington has taken the '32 Ford Roadster and refined the lines, making it look as if it were designed by one of the major automotive studios. The *Boydster 1* was a highboy and the *Boydster 2* was full-fendered.

Even Lexus built a version of the '32 Roadster. This car debuted at the 1998 Los Angeles Auto Show and was designed to showcase the Lexus GS400 V-8 engine.

THE FUTURE OF THE 1932 FORD

Don Prieto can attest that driving the Lexus-powered roadster can be fun. The interior is trimmed in leather and the transmission is a six-speed manual.

The future of the 1932 Ford is brighter than ever. More and more people are finding out how enjoyable hot rodding is and how nice the people are who participate in the hobby. The creation of reproduction bodies has expanded the availability of hot rodding to anyone who wants one. While reproduction bodies were once thought of as the end of the value of hot rods and original vintage cars, these reproduction cars have only increased the demand for, and prices of, original bodies. This interest in reproduction '32 Ford bodies has also pushed the envelope of hot rod design. Today, anyone can build a hot rod in his own garage or go to one of the many quality builders and spec out a hot rod. With turnkey hot rods available and with the corporate involvement of GM and DaimlerChrysler to produce limited edition cars for the 75th anniversary, 2007 should be an exciting year. The future is bright for the Deuce and many of us hope we're still alive to celebrate the 100th anniversary of the 1932 Ford.

Lexus started with a 300-horsepower, 4.0 liter V-8 with 32 valves and four cams with continuous variable timing. Toyota engineers added an extra 100 horsepower through the use of an off-road intake manifold and a small change in cam timing. The pushrod/rocker-style front suspension is patterned after an Indy car.

187 ■ DEUCE: 75 YEARS OF THE '32 FORD

The future of the '32 Ford can be seen in Jerry Jacobson's low-slung roadster. The look is long and low. Not only has the frame been stretched, but the character line also has been changed to continue along the entire length of the rail. Air suspension controls the ride height.

The grille shell on Jacobson's roadster is traditional '32 Ford, but the insert is a custom-made billet piece. The headlights are mounted low on continuations of the nerf bar that protects the lower edge of the grille shell.

PHOTO CREDITS

From the Collections of The Henry Ford:
10 (upper), 11 (lower), 12, 13 (lower), 30 (lower), 33 (top), 42 (lower), 43 (upper), 57, 60, 61 (both), 62 (bottom), 63 (lower), 66, 74 (both), 75 (both), 76, 77 (lower), 79 (both), 103, 104, 138 (both), 139 (top), 141 (top), 144 (bottom), 145, 146 (both), 154 (upper right), 156 (upper & lower left)

Author collection:
10 (lower), 11 (upper), 20, 22, 23 (both), 24, 25 (both), 26, 27, 31 (upper left), 109 (upper left), 112 (bottom)

David Newhardt:
28, 155 (lower)

Kevin Lee:
131

American Hot Rod Foundation:
82, 83, 88 (both), 133 (bottom right), 167 (lower)

Brookville:
176 (top right)

Hot Rods and Horsepower:
177, 178 (top), 179 (bottom), 180, 181 (both), 182, 183 (both)

Speedway Motors:
184, 185 (both)

INDEX

A

Alexander Brothers, 123, 126-127
Allison, Jamie, 181
Alvarez, Julian, 7, 147
Ambassador Bridge, 159
Amber Trakul, 6
American Graffiti, 4, 16, 19, 113-116, 122-123, 130
AMT, 162
Ardun heads, 67
Asquith, Boyce, 130
Astor, Henry, 7, 168
Austin, Jim, 7, 100, 117
Autorama, 16, 124, 157

B

B-400, 37, 42, 77, 143-145
B-model, 75
Barris, George, 127, 129
Baskerville, Gray, 130-131
Bauder, Bob, 7, 127, 164
Beach Boys, 122, 124, 129
Beatnik Bandit, 192
Beck, Jeff, 130
Berardini brothers, 95, 100
Berardini, Tony, 94, 98
Bergren, Dick, 135
Berry, Bob, 7, 171
Boden, John, 7
Bonneville, 67, 130
Boss 429, 192
Boule, David, 7, 17, 132
Bow Tie Deuce, 182, 185-186
Boydster I, 130
Breece, Bill, 130
Brizio, Andy, 130
Brizio, Roy, 130
Brooks, Phil, 7, 172
Brookville, 7, 173-179
Brown, Ray, 130
Burnett, Brian, 130
Buttera, John, 130

C

C. R. Wilson Carriage Company, 21
Cabriolet, 10, 12, 37-38, 48, 50, 75, 77-79, 88, 145, 177, 179
Cadillac, 22, 57, 186
Capitol Records, 129
Carpenter, Don, 7, 167
Catallo, Chili, 17, 122, 124, 130, 133
Catallo, Curt, 7, 133

Chapouris, Pete, 7, 97, 130
Charger, 185
Chevrolet, 8, 26, 29, 31, 57, 68, 75, 116, 120, 129, 162, 169, 181-183, 187
Chrysler, 162, 183-185
Chrysler Deuce, 184-185
Clark, Don, 67
Cleveland, 152
Cobra, 180, 183, 192
Coddington, Boyd, 130
Conway, Junior, 127
Cool, Phil, 130
Corvette, 161, 167, 185-187
Couch, Bill, 7, 84
Couch, John, 7, 165
Couzens, James, 21-22
Cronin, Rick, 7
Crouse, Dave, 95

D

DaimlerChrysler, 180-181, 183-184, 187
Davis, Sam, 7, 122
de Heras, Chuck, 7, 160, 163-164
de Heras, Derek, 7
De Angelis, George, 7
Dearborn Deuce, 79, 177-185
Delco, 46, 49
Deluxe, 10, 12-13, 31, 33-34, 37, 40, 44, 47-48, 50, 52, 70-72, 74-75, 77-81, 102-104, 108-110, 112, 137-141, 143-145, 154, 156
Desatoff, Bill, 130
Desbrow, Roy, 130
Detroit, 16, 21-22, 59, 66, 84, 120, 123-124, 126, 152, 156-157, 159-163, 179
Dodge Brothers, 21
Duesenberg, 36, 57
Duntov, Yura, 65

E

Earl, Harley, 26
East, Neal, 16, 97, 130
Eastwood, Pete, 164
Edelbrock, Vic, 19, 130
Edison Illuminating Company, 21
Edison, Thomas, 60
Elvis, 171
Erickson, Larry, 181
Everet, Bob, 119
Everets, Bob, 7, 98

F

Falfa, Bob, 123
Farrar, John, 7
Ferrari, Dean, 7
Figari, Rick, 7, 116, 123
Fink, Dan, 130
Fish, Randy, 7, 98
Five-window, 18, 37, 44, 47, 64, 102-110, 112-120, 122-123, 141, 162, 165, 176
Flathead, 19, 64-68, 82, 87, 90, 94-96, 100, 118, 134, 157, 161
Ford, Edsel, 27, 130
Ford, Harrison, 123
Ford, Henry, 7, 9, 21-25, 27, 29, 37, 40, 46, 57-63, 65, 78, 130, 148, 150, 175-176
Foster, Tommy, 130
Franklin, Johnny, 120

G

Gammel, Doyle, 127, 133
General Mills, 162
General Motors, 26, 180, 183, 185-187
Gilles, Ralph, 184
Gingerelli, Dain, 7
Gollahon, Ray, 175
Gommi, Paul, 7, 97, 155
Graves, Richard, 130
Greene, Bob, 127
Gross, Ken, 7, 85, 130, 133, 192
Guasco, Rich, 7, 120

H

Hall, Jon, 7, 64, 99, 118, 163
Hamilton, Bob, 117
Hanley, John, 162
Hemi, 15, 65, 98, 118, 181, 184-185
Henderson, Wayne, 130

I

Immerso, Ermie, 130

J

Jacobson, Jerry, 7, 188
Jankowski, Gary, 7

K

Kassa, Andy, 130
Kessler, Gary, 130
Khougaz, Jim, 130

INDEX

King, Paul, 7
Kirby, Mark, 7, 64
Knight, Craig, 7
Kolmos, Bob, 130
Kugel, Jerry, 130
Kuttner, Jack, 7, 170
Kyle, Dennis, 130

L

Laird, Ray, 60
Larivee, Bob, 133
Lee, Kevin, 131
LeMat, Paul, 120
Lexus, 186-187
Lincoln, 4, 27, 34, 57, 96, 124
Little Deuce Coupe, 130
Lobeck, Barry, 7
Lucas, George, 115, 117
Luzader, Harry, 130

M

Malcomson, Alexander, 21-22
Marquez, Dave, 130
Martin, Mike, 130
Masa, Tony La, 130
Maynard, John, 7, 100
McGee, Bob, 89-91, 97-98
McMullen, Tom, 130, 135
Messer, Dick, 7
Meyer, Bruce, 7, 94, 97, 127, 130
Meyer, Fred, 7
Miller, Ak, 130
Milner, John, 16, 114, 116, 120
Model A, 4-5, 9, 15, 20-27, 29, 32, 34, 36-40, 43, 45, 47, 54, 57, 59, 63-65, 67-69, 72, 74-75, 78, 90, 92, 103-106, 112, 137, 139, 141, 151-152, 154, 156, 162-163, 175, 177, 179
Model T, 9, 20, 22-24, 26, 40, 57, 63, 89-90, 103
Moeller, Bill, 16
Mopar, 133, 181
More American Graffiti, 116, 123
Morris, Bob, 130
Morrison, Roger, 7, 95
Mountanos, Mark, 7

N

NASCAR, 162
Newhardt, David, 7, 155
NHRA, 160
Nitti, Joe, 121, 130

O

Oldsmobile, 57-58, 124
Orr, Jim, 7

P

Pankow, Kerry, 169
Park, Allen, 124, 126
Petersen Automotive Museum, 7, 28, 133
Peterson, Elwood, 7, 165
Phaeton, 10, 31, 48, 50, 71, 78-81, 130, 145, 173
Plymouth, 29, 75, 126-127
Pontiac, 58, 93, 162
Price, Chuck, 130
Prieto, Don, 6-7, 172, 187
Prufer, Tom, 130

R

Rehor, David, 7
Rickman, Eric, 127
Ritzow, Roger, 130
Roadster, 6-7, 15-16, 19, 22, 25, 31, 33, 42, 48, 50, 67, 70-75, 78-100, 107, 121, 130-131, 135, 145, 153, 155, 159, 162-163, 172-177, 179-180, 184-188
Robinson, Mark, 181
Rod & Custom, 16, 127, 135, 162
Rothenberg, Bob, 130
Rudolph, Janice, 7

S

Schultz, Carl, 60
Scritchfield, Dick, 94, 130
SCTA, 15, 82, 85, 89
Sedan, 4, 10, 12-13, 27, 31, 33-34, 37-38, 44-45, 48, 50, 71, 77, 82, 85, 103, 130, 136-149, 157-165, 167-169, 192
Sedan Delivery, 31, 33-34, 45, 48, 145-149, 158
Sein, George, 130
Seleski, Jim, 156, 158-159
Sharp, Greg, 7
Shelby, Carroll, 180, 183
Shelton, Jim, 131
Simard, Dave, 85
Siroonian, John, 130
Smith, Bill, 7, 184, 187
SoCal Speed Shop, 7
Southard, Andy, 135
Speedway Motors, 7, 184-185, 187
Spencer, Doane, 91-94, 97, 130
Sport Coupe, 10, 31, 38, 48, 50, 103-105, 130, 143, 145
Standard, 6, 10, 13, 30, 37, 40, 47-48, 50, 52, 68, 71-72, 74-75, 77-81, 102-106, 108-110, 136-140, 143, 148, 151-154, 156
Stringer, Lynn, 7

T

Tebow, Clem, 67
Thacker, Tony, 7
Thelen, Don, 130
Thoms, Fred, 57
Three-window, 17, 31, 33-34, 37, 102-104, 108-112, 122, 124, 127, 129, 132-133, 135, 170-173, 176-179
Toteff, George, 162
Toyota, 187
Trakul, Amber, 6

U

Universal Studios, 116, 122

V

V-8, 4-5, 8-11, 15-16, 19, 28-31, 38, 40, 45-50, 52, 54, 56-69, 75, 79-80, 82, 96, 102, 107, 112, 124, 130, 136-137, 140-141, 145, 155, 162, 186-187
Van Hoff, Don, 130
VanBuskirk, Dr. Mark, 7
Victoria, 10, 12, 31, 34, 36-37, 44, 48, 50, 55, 103, 141-143, 145, 167
Von Dutch, 100, 192

W

Wescott, Dee, 172
Whitney, J. C., 159, 163
Williams, Robert, 192
Willis, C. Harold, 21
Wineland, Lynn, 97
Woloszak, Ray, 133
Woodward, Bill, 16
World War II, 16, 29, 82, 93, 136

Z

Zoerlein, Emil, 60

More GREAT Titles from CarTech®...

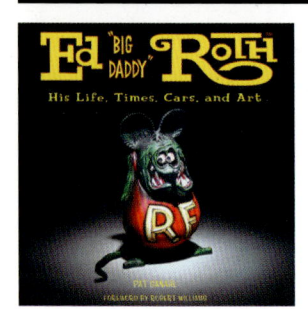

ED "BIG DADDY" ROTH: HIS LIFE, TIMES, CARS AND ART by Pat Ganahl. Foreword by artist Robert Williams. Who was Ed Roth? The answer depends on who you ask, and when they knew him. To some, he was a counter-culture, greasy-fingernailed, renaissance man of the mid 20th Century. To others, he's the creator of Rat Fink and builder of some of the most creative custom cars ever to get a coat of candy paint – cars like the *Beatnik Bandit*, the *Mysterion*, and the *Outlaw*. Ed's rise to fame began in the '50s, and peaked with the custom car boom of the early '60s – every kid in America knew who Rat Fink was, and many built models of his custom cars and wore his "monster" T-shirts. To say his life was interesting is an understatement – and this book covers it all, from art to custom cars, monster shirts to VW-powered trikes, and the wild life that brought it all together. Hardbound, 10 x 10 inches, 192 pages, 100 color photos, 150 B&W photos. *Item # CT968*

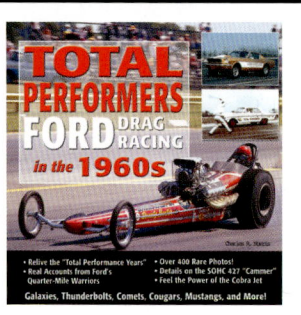

TOTAL PERFORMERS: Ford Drag Racing in the 1960s by Charles Morris. The 1960s was arguably the most important decade for drag racing. Among the best high-performance cars & engines were those coming from Dearborn, Michigan. Ford Motor Company's "Total Performance Years" saw a breakthrough as drag racing helped the younger, performance- and style-conscious consumer to begin receiving some recognition. Factory participation in drag racing pushed the envelope for high performance developments. Ford's FE-series engine, Police Interceptor, GT 390, Single Overhead Cam, Cobra Jet, and Boss 429 are all covered in detail. See the cars and the drivers that made them famous. Hardbound, 10 x 10 inches, 192 pages, 130 color photos & 290 B/W photos. *Item #CT407*

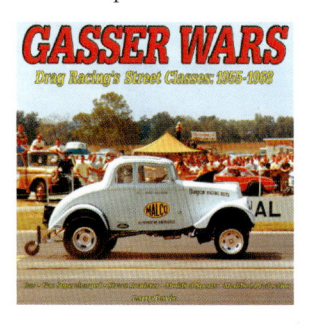

GASSER WARS: DRAG RACING'S STREET CLASSES: 1955-1968 by Larry Davis. In the late '50s, thousands of street legal hot rods participated in organized drag races across the country – they ran in three major categories: Gas, Modified Production & Modified Sports. As racers got more serious & car manufacturers began sponsoring cars & touting their accomplishments in ads, the "Gasser Wars" were born. This book covers the '60s most exciting drag racing classes in detail, with vintage never-before-seen photos of VERY rare versions of the cars that raced during this era. This is the ONLY book on the subject currently in the marketplace! Hardbound, 10 x 10 inches, 192 pages, 100 color photos, 200 B&W photos. *Item # CT977*

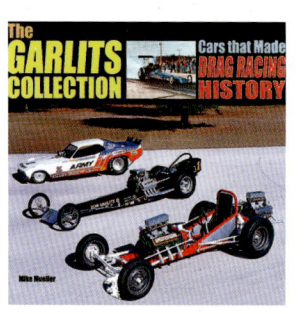

THE GARLITS COLLECTION by Mike Mueller. It isn't just his racing accomplishments that set Don "Big Daddy" Garlits apart in drag racing history. This is a man who truly loves drag racing, and on his own he has constructed one of the best motorsports museums in the world – The Don Garlits Museum of Drag Racing, in Ocala, Florida. His museum contains hundreds of cars, but in this book, author Mike Mueller takes an in-depth look at the cream of the crop – the most significant cars in Big Daddy's museum, and probably the most significant cars in all of drag racing. Funny cars, Pro/Stocks, Fuel Coupes, roadsters, streamliners, Super Stocks, Gassers and more – this book covers them all, with spectacular color photos of the restored machines, right alongside vintage black-and-white images from Garlits' own collection. Hardbound, 10 x 10 inches, 192 pages, close to 300 color & B/W photos. *Item # CT981*

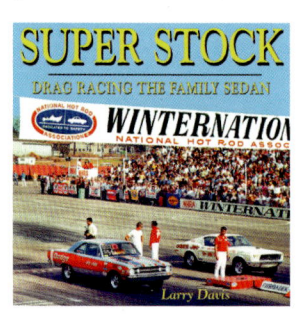

SUPER STOCK: DRAG RACING THE FAMILY SEDAN by Larry Davis. This book takes a look at what was, in the 1960s, the most popular class of drag racing – factory Super Stock. It traces the evolution of the cars, the engines, the rules, the personalities, and many of the teams, from its beginnings in the mid-1950s through to the 1960s. This was the period that saw emergence of the term "musclecar" and the production of a whole class of American automobiles. Includes first-person accounts of what drag racing was really like in the early 1960s: how the manufacturers controlled the competition and even race results, and how the sanctioning bodies attempted to control the manufacturers, who in turn simply sidestepped the rules. Appendices include the major event winners and the rules defining the classes as well as information detailing the engines and chassis in Top Stock categories. Hardbound, 10 x 10 inches, 216 pages, 33 color photos, 300 B&W photos. *Item # CT953*

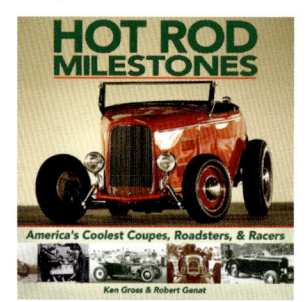

HOT ROD MILESTONES by Ken Gross & Robert Genat. You've seen these cars before. They're some of the best-known, coolest hot rods ever built. Each represents a clear vision, usually from one talented person. These hot rods set the standards; they were imitated, and when they made show appearances, they were coveted and revered. *Hot Rod Milestones* covers 25 of the most influential, innovative hot rods ever built from the late 1940s to the mid '60s. Each car's history, technical background, and influence is discussed, along with information on the builders and owners. Photos include contemporary pictures of the cars as they exist now, along with vintage photos of the cars when they were first built and shown. Hardbound, 10 x 10 inches, 150 color & 100 B/W photos. *Item # CT980*

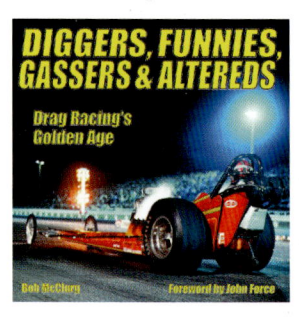

DIGGERS, FUNNIES, GASSERS & ALTEREDS: Drag Racing's Golden Era by Bob McClurg. During the '60s, drag racing evolved from a grass roots effort to a full-blown professional motorsport – along the way, it created some of the most exciting racing & race cars ever built. Bob McClurg, an accomplished magazine writer & photographer, is best known for his drag racing images of the '60s and '70s – his lens captured the Roadsters, Gassers, Altereds, Top Fuelers, Funny Cars, Pro/Stocks, & even the modern age of nostalgia drag racing. With more than 350 color and black-and-white photos, this book is an exciting visual history of the Golden Age of drag racing. Hardbound, 10 x 10 inches, 192 pages, 200 color photos, 150 B&W photos. *Item# CT990*

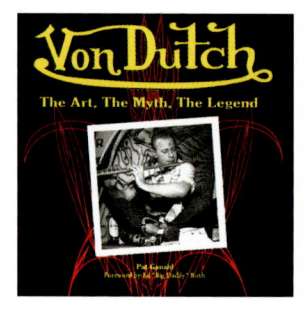

VON DUTCH: THE ART, THE MYTH, THE LEGEND by Pat Ganahl. Von Dutch is one of the most interesting characters in hot rod and popular culture history. Considered the founder of "modern" pinstriping, he was a prominent character in many of the rodding magazines of the late '50s, and his fame endured long after he apparently tired of it. Besides being a striper, he was a gifted artist, machinist, and gun- and knife-smith. Using stories and quotes culled from interviews, vintage photos, and images of the art and other works he left behind, this book chronicles Kenneth Howard's life from pinstriping beatnik to bus-dwelling hermit. Where it can, this book sets the record straight on Von Dutch the man, but in many cases conflicting stories will serve to illustrate the contrary, colorful, and sometimes difficult nature of Von Dutch the legend. This book is a must-have for fans of hot rodding and hot rod culture! Hardbound, 10 x 10 inches, 192 pages, 100 color & 200 B/W photos. *Item # CT998*

CarTech®, Inc., 39966 Grand Avenue, North Branch, MN 55056
Telephone: (651) 277-1200 or (800) 551-4754 Fax: (651) 277-1203, www.cartechbooks.com

More great titles available from CarTech®...

S-A DESIGN

Ford Performance — Practical building tips, for all Ford V-8 engines. (SA05)

Smokey Yunick's Power Secrets — Smokey explains race-engine prep from carbs to shop tools. (SA06)

Small-Block Chevy Performance, Vol 1: 1955-81 — Block, head selection & prep., ignition, carb & more! (SA07)

Super Tuning & Modifying Holley Carburetors — Perf, street and off-road applications. (SA08)

Custom Painting — The Do-It-Yourself Guide to – Advice on choosing paint, prep and touch-up. (SA10)

Super Tuning and Modifying Carter Carburetors — Tuning and modifying for power or economy. (SA11)

Street Supercharging, The Complete Guide to — Bolt-on buying, installing and tuning blowers. (SA17)

Engine Blueprinting — Using tools, block selection & prep, crank mods, pistons, heads, cams & more! (SA21)

How to Build Horsepower, Vol. 1 — Building horsepower in any engine. (SA24)

Super '60s Fords — The inside story of the most powerful Fords ever built from 1957-1973. (SA25)

How To Rebuild the Small-Block Chevrolet — How to build a street or racing small-block Chevy. (SA26)

Holley Rebuilding and Modifying — Tuning, modifying, and rebuilding all Holley modular carbs. (SA27)

Chevrolet Big-Block Parts Interchange Manual — Selecting & swapping high-perf. big-block parts. (SA31)

High-Perf Crate Motor Buyer's Guide — Complete guide to all factory & aftermarket high-perf engines. (SA32)

How To Design & Install High Performance Car Stereo — A beginner's guide to high-tech sound systems. (SA45)

How To Build Max Performance Chevy Rat Motors — Hot rodding big-block Chevys. (SA48)

High Performance Honda Builder's Handbook Vol. 1 — How to build & tune high-performance Honda cars and engines. (SA49)

How To Install & Use Nitrous Oxide — How to make max power with nitrous oxide injection. (SA50)

Desktop Dynos — Using computers to build & test engines. (SA51)

How To Build Horsepower, V.2 — Carbs & intake manifolds. (SA52)

Chevrolet TPI Fuel Injection Swappers Guide — Interchanging & modifying TPI systems. (SA53)

The 5.0L Mustang Bolt-On Performance Guide — Covers Mustangs from 1979 -1995. (SA54)

Chevrolet Small-Block Parts Interchange Manual — Selecting & swapping high-perf. small-block parts. (SA55)

High-Performance Ford Engine Parts Interchange — Selecting & swapping big- and small-block Ford parts. (SA56)

How To Build Max Perf Chevy Small-Blocks on a Budget — Would you believe 600 hp for $3000? (SA57)

High-Performance Honda Builder's Handbook Vol. 2 — Suspensions, body mods, brake tech, nitrous. (SA58)

Chrysler Performance Upgrades — Performance improvements on Chrysler muscle cars of the '60s & '70s. (SA60)

5.0L Ford Dyno Tests — Data from over 2000 dyno pulls on aftermarket bolt-on performance parts. (SA61)

Building Ford Short-Track Power, Official Factory Guide to — Written by Ford Racing engineers. (SA63)

Sport Compact Bolt-On Perf Guide, Vol 1: Import Cars — A catalog of aftermarket components for imports. (SA65)

How To Build High-Performance Chrysler Engines — Parts interchanges, factory crate motors, cylinder heads, etc. (SA67)

How To Tune and Win With Demon Carburetors — Selecting and tuning for high-perf race, street, & off-road applications. (SA68)

How To Build Max Performance Ford V-8s on a Budget — Dyno-tested engine builds for big- & small-block Fords. (SA69)

How To Build Honda Horsepower — Data from 1000s of dyno pulls on aftermarket perf parts and mods for Hondas. (SA71)

Sport Compact Nitrous Injection — Expert tuning tips for installing and tuning NOS systems on tuners. (SA73)

Building High-Perf Fox-Body Mustangs on a Budget — Building the complete package. Covers 1979-95 5.0L Mustangs. (SA75)

How To Build Max-Perf Pontiac V8s — Mild perf apps to all-out performance build-ups. (SA78)

How To Build High-Performance Ignition Systems — Complete guide to understanding auto ignition systems. (SA79)

How To Build & Modify GM Pro Touring Street Machines — Classic looks with modern performance. (SA81)

How To Build Max Perf 4.6 Liter Ford Engines — Building & modifying Ford's 2- and 4-valve 4.6/5.4 liter engines. (SA82)

Building & Tuning High-Perf Electronic Fuel Injection — Custom engine management systems for domestics & imports. (SA83)

How To Build Big-Inch Ford Small-Blocks — Add cubic inches without the hassle of switching to a big-block. (SA85)

How To Build High-Perf Chevy LS1/LS6 Engines — Modifying and tuning Gen-III engines for GM cars and trucks. (SA86)

How To Build Big-Inch Chevy Small-Blocks — Get the additional torque & horsepower of a big-block. (SA87)

Harley-Davidson Bolt-On Performance — Max performance for Big-Twins and Sportsters motorcycles. (SA88)

Sport Compact Turbos & Blowers — Guide to understanding, installing, & using sport compact turbos & superchargers. (SA89)

Ford Focus Builder's Handbook — Data from 100s of dyno runs on aftermarket perf parts and modifications. (SA90)

Six-Pack: Mopar Street Muscle in the '60s — Development history, tuning & modifying, tech information. (SA92)

Honda Engine Swaps — Step-by-step instructions for all major tasks involved in engine swapping. (SA93)

How to Build Supercharged & Turbocharged Small-Block Fords — Everything you need to know about supercharging & turbocharging your small-block Ford. (SA95)

High-Performance Pontiacs 1955-1974 — Covers the best years of Pontiac, including GTO & Firebird as well as Wide Track, Trans-Am, Bonneville, Tri-Power, & Grand Prix. (SA96)

Quarter-Mile Muscle: Detroit Goes to the Drags — Covers the development & success of muscle cars at the drags in all classes in the '60s. (SA98)

High-Performance Dodge Neon Builder's Handbook — Everything you need to know to get maximum performance out of your Dodge Neon. (SA100)

How to Build Ford Restomod Street Machines — Modify your vintage Ford to accelerate, stop, corner & ride like a new high-performance car. (SA101)

How to Rebuild the Small-Block Ford — Covers a small-block Ford rebuild step by step, including planning, disassembly & inspection, choosing parts, machine work, assembly, first firing & break-in. (SA102)

How to Build Big-Inch Mopar Small Blocks — How to get big-block power out of your Mopar small-block. (SA104)

How to Build High-Performance Chevy Small — Block Cams/Valvetrains — Camshaft & valvetrain function, selection, performance, and design. (SA105)

High-Performance Mustang Builder's Guide 1994-2004 — Build your Mustang for drag racing, road racing, or improved street performance. (SA106)

High-Performance Honda & Acura Buyer's Guide — How to buy the right Honda/Acura to modify for performance. (SA108)

High-Performance Jeep Cherokee XJ Builder's Guide 1984-2001 — Build a useful, Cherokee for mountains, the mud, the desert, the street, and more. (SA109)

High-Performance Ford Mustang Buyer's Guide: 1979 – Present — Guidance on buying the right Mustang to modify for performance. (SA111)

How to Build and Modify Rochester Quadrajet Carburetors — Selecting, rebuilding, and modifying the Quadrajet Carburetors. (SA113)

Building 4.6/5.4L Ford Horsepower on the Dyno — Takes the guesswork out of choosing parts by providing horsepower & torque gains expected from each modification. (SA115)

Rebuilding the Small-Block Chevy: Step-by-Step Videobook — 160-pg book plus 2-hour DVD show you how to build a street or racing small-block Chevy. (SA116)

How to Paint Your Car on a Budget — Everything you need to know to get a great-looking coat of paint and save money. (SA117)

HISTORIES AND PERSONALITIES

Total Performers: Ford Drag Racing in the 1960s — Covers Ford Motor Company's "Total Performance Years" in 1960s drag racing. See the cars & the drivers that made them famous. (CT407)

NASCAR's Wild Years — Stock-Car technology in the '60s includes the behind-the-scenes battles between factories, rule-makers, track owners, promoters, & racing teams. (CT409)

Quarter-Mile Chaos — Rare & stunning photos of terrifying fires, explosions, and crashes in drag racing's golden age. (CT425)

Super Stock: Drag Racing the Family Sedan — Takes a look at the '60s most popular class of drag racing — factory Super Stock. (CT953)

Ed "Big Daddy" Roth: His Life, Times, Cars and Art — The creator of Rat Fink had a profound influence on hot rodders and popular culture. (CT968)

Gasser Wars — Drag Racing's Street Classes: 1955-1968 — An entertaining look into the most exciting drag racing action of the '50s and '60s. (CT977)

Diggers, Funnies, Gassers & Altereds — An exciting visual history of the Golden Age of drag racing. 10 x 10, hdbd. 192 pages. (CT990)

Indy's Wildest Decade: Innovation and Revolution at the Brickyard — Year-by-year account of Indy's wildest decade, the 1960s. (CT971)

The Garlits Collection: Cars that Made Drag Racing History — Coverage of the most significant cars in Big Daddy's museum. (CT981)

Hot Rod Milestones: America's Coolest Coupes, Roadsters, & Racers — Covers 25 of the most influential, innovative hot rods ever built from the late '40s to the mid '60s. (CT980)

Von Dutch: The Art, The Myth, The Legend — Chronicles the life & art of pinstriper Von Dutch, from his days as a pinstriping beatnik to bus-dwelling hermit. (CT998)

CarTech®, Inc. 30966 Grand Ave, North Branch, MN 55056. Ph: 800-551-4754 or 651-277-1200 • Fax: 651-277-1203

Brooklands Books Ltd., PO Box 146 Cobham, Surrey KT11 1LG, England. Ph: 01932 865051, Fax 01932 868803

Brooklands Books Aus., 3/37-39 Green Street, Banksmeadow, NSW 2019, Australia. Ph: 2 9695 7055 Fax 2 9695 7355

Visit us online at www.cartechbooks.com for more info!